Policing within the Law

Policing within the Law
A Case Study of the New York City Police Department

JOHN ETERNO

Westport, Connecticut
London

Library of Congress Cataloging-in-Publication Data

Eterno, John, 1959–
    Policing within the law : a case study of the New York City Police Department / John
Eterno.
        p. cm.
    Includes bibliographical references and index.
    ISBN 0-275-97592-4 (alk. paper)
    1. New York (N.Y.) Police Dept.—Decision making.   2. Police-community relations—
New York (State)—New York.   3. Police power—New York (State)—New York.
4. Police administration—New York (State)—New York.   I. Title.
HV8148.N5E84   2003
363.2′09747′1—dc21   2002037059

British Library Cataloguing in Publication Data is available.

Library of Congress Catalog Card Number: 2002037059
ISBN: 0-275-97592-4

First published in 2003

Praeger Publishers, 88 Post Road West, Westport, CT 06881
An imprint of Greenwood Publishing Group, Inc.
www.praeger.com

Printed in the United States of America

The paper used in this book complies with the
Permanent Paper Standard issued by the National
Information Standards Organization (Z39.48–1984).

P

Copyright Acknowledgments

A small part of the materials contained in this volume herein were originally published as a
refereed (i.e., peer reviewed) journal article authored by the undersigned. Parts are reprinted
in this book with the permission of *Police Practice and Research: An International Journal,*
published by OPA (Overseas Publishers Association), N.V. Published by license under the
Harwood Academic Publishers imprint, part of the Gordon and Breach Publishing Group. The
article is cited as:
Eterno, John A. (2001). "Zero Tolerance Policing in Democracies: The Dilemma of Controlling
Crime Without Increasing Police Abuse of Power." *Police Practice and Research: An International Journal* Vol. 2(3), pp. 189–217.

To my wife, JoAnn, and daughter, Julia

Contents

Acknowledgments

An endeavor of this magnitude would have been impossible without the assistance of many others. Some of these are police contacts I have met over the years, and others are academics who have studied in this field for many years. Of course, there are so many who have contributed that it would be impossible to list them all. Please forgive me if I missed someone—there are just so many. The contributions made by the people whose names follow are not merely to this work; they have all, in their own way, enriched and touched my life making me a better individual. First and foremost on the list is my wife, JoAnn. Her tireless efforts in reading and suggesting changes, watching our newborn baby, going to school, and making our home livable are incredible. My other family members, too, were a tremendous help, including my mom, Teresa, and my brother, James, whose critique of this manuscript was incredibly annoying but very helpful. Of course, James, I owe it all to you.

Professor Eli Silverman of John Jay College, City University of New York, has been a constant inspiration and help. His vast knowledge of the New York City Police Department (NYPD) and his academic background made him ideally suited to assisting me. His reading and editorial comments were especially noteworthy. Thank you, Eli. Professors Vincent Henry (Pace University) and Chris Sullivan (Molloy College), both former colleagues at the NYPD, also were very knowledgeable and extremely helpful.

At the University at Albany, State University of New York, there were many supportive people. Professor Robert E. Worden's vast knowledge of policing administration and methods was especially helpful. Professor M. Craig Brown's expertise in research design and statistics was critical, especially with regard to the questionnaire. Professor James Acker's legal knowledge was indispensable. Professor Fred Cohen, who gave me the sparks that ignited this work so many years ago, was an exceptional mentor. Professor David Bayley, who assisted by reading, commenting, and evaluating materials at various stages, was invaluable. Furthermore, I must thank Andie Lawrence, Charlie Lanier, and Mark Gorthy for being good friends and helping with ideas.

The Police Foundation and the NYPD have been very supportive—in particular, Deputy Commissioner Michael J. Farrell, Assistant Commissioner Philip G. McGuire, Assistant Chief Joanne Jaffe, retired Captain William Chimento, Captain William Mahaney, Lieutenant James Ranelli, retired Lieutenant James O'Brien, and Sergeant Martin Gleeson.

The NYPD was open to being studied and gave me permission to conduct this comprehensive investigation. To them I am forever thankful. The NYPD, however, is not responsible for any content contained in this book. These ideas are mine, and I take full and complete responsibility for its contents.

A special thanks to Dr. Peter Rossi for his guidance and computer program. Speaking of computers—no, I did not forget you, Danny Srebnick. Thanks to both a friend and one of the most knowledgeable people I know when it comes to computers.

The International Police Executive Symposium has given me contacts in policing throughout the world, as well as opportunities that I thought would never be possible. In particular, I would like to thank Professors Dilip Das and Arvind Verma. They have been an invaluable source of information, inspiration, and assistance.

I must also thank the clergy and staff of Saint Andrew's in New York City, Our Lady of the Blessed Sacrament in New York City, and Our Lady of the Angels in Albany. To all who have helped, thanks for your prayers, support, and love. May God bless all of you and those you love.

Preface

This book is the by-product of more than twenty years of practical experience as a sworn law enforcement officer as well as many years of intensive academic research on police. Practical experience permits a researcher to develop relationships such that close observation of subjects in the field environment, and candid discussion and direct interaction, are possible without subjects' changing their behavior. For example, observational research (especially on sensitive topics such as those studied in this work) can be tainted by what social scientists call the Hawthorne effect (subjects changing their behavior because they are aware that they are being observed). Practical experience helps to prevent this effect. Indeed, practical experience, without more, would be enough to develop a basic understanding of how police behave.

However, in order to measure and understand these experiences more accurately, the use of social science research practices are utilized extensively. The cornerstone of these methods is a scientifically designed questionnaire that took years to develop. It involved, for example, the use of focus groups, pretesting the instrument, and using statistical tests to ensure the instrument was accurately measuring and capturing the behavior of officers. This combination of experience and social science methods allows for a more accurate understanding of police behavior.

Introduction

Most of us think of the police as crime fighters. Indeed, when we think of a police officer, many of us conjure up images of gunfights and car chases. This stereotypical image of the cop as a crime fighter is perpetuated by modern media portrayals of police. Who cannot recall films with exciting car chases or fights where the good guy cop is battling a notorious criminal? Certainly one important aspect of policing is crime-fighting: preventing and detecting crime, making arrests, writing summonses, and the like. Unfortunately, this crime-fighting image of police is so patently incomplete that it absolutely blinds many people to a more accurate picture of police. In fact, many police academies valiantly attempt to eradicate these images from recruits' minds in order to prevent them from doing the behaviors seen in these media portrayals, such as wild car chases.

The aim of this book is to unveil a relatively hidden but equally important aspect of policing. In particular, the objective is to demonstrate that controlling police abuse of authority is just as important to the mission of policing as controlling crime is. Many, including current police officers and leaders, neither fully appreciate nor completely understand this aspect of policing. Yet it is precisely this other side that separates police officers in democratic countries from those in totalitarian regimes and from terrorists. Using practical experience based on more than twenty years with the New York City Police Department and social science methods learned through many years of education, as well as through experience as a consultant and conducting research for the NYPD, in this work I explain in rudimentary terms the dynamics of how the law attempts to limit police behavior.

To begin to understand these dynamics, one must realize that the power of police can be enormous, especially in times of fear and anxiety.

In fact, it is clear that in the current times, very aggressive crime-fighting strategies will be necessary to battle crime and terrorism. Areas in which the police are more likely to abuse their authority will be outlined. Additionally, practical suggestions for dealing with these areas of concern are fully explained.

Professionals in law enforcement, the law, and the social sciences—as well as general readers—will learn from this book how police act, and should act, in a free society. This work also presents a twofold challenge to policymakers, lawmakers, law enforcement officers, and others interested in police work. First, to comprehend the significant ramifications of aggressive crime control policies that empower police to fight crime. Second, based on this understanding, to develop and act on policies that properly check and balance increased officer authority such that we can all live in a free society.

Chapter 1

The Police, the Law, and Behavior

The terrorist attacks leading to the collapse of the World Trade Center killed thousands and touched the lives of countless others. In New York City on September 11, 2001, the beauty of a sunny, late summer day was darkened by the debris and dust that were the remains of those awesome structures now reduced to ashes. People were stunned as death unexpectedly lurked near. Lives were changed forever. Fear, above all, seemed to rule. Issues that seemed important only a day earlier now became meaningless. In these turbulent times one can only ponder the extent to which power will be ascribed to law enforcement to forestall the recurrence of anything that even remotely comes close to these tragic events.

As a start, on September 14, 2001, Congress passed a resolution giving the President authority "to use 'all necessary and appropriate force' against international terrorism" (Glaberson, 2001: B6). Further, on October 26, 2001, President George W. Bush signed legislation aimed at fighting terrorism entitled Uniting and Strengthening America by providing Appropriate Tools Required to Intercept and Obstruct Terrorism (shortened to the USA PATRIOT ACT of 2001) (see Clymer, 2001: B5). The American Civil Liberties Union expressed concern that the vast powers conferred could be abused by law enforcement. Nevertheless, the public, at least initially, was quite supportive of the president. However, between December 7 and December 10, 2001, when asked in a nationwide *New York Times*/CBS poll "what worried them more—that the government would fail to enact strong antiterrorism laws or that the government would enact new antiterrorism laws that excessively restrict the average person's civil liberties—Americans were evenly divided, 43 to 45 percent" (Toner and Elder, 2001: A1).

At the international level, this issue has also come to the forefront. For example, in India an antiterrorism law was passed after enormous debate that involved "shouts and appeals for calm from the speaker of the house" (Sengupta, 2002: A5). Concern over what is called the Prevention of Terrorism Ordinance is focused on whether the law "would be used against ordinary citizens and religious minorities" (Sengupta, 2002: A5). The new law grants police considerable authority to combat terrorist activities. One example of these vastly expanded powers is the ability of police to hold those suspected of terrorist activities for ninety days without a trial. Those who favor the law argue that it is necessary to help prevent future terrorist activities. However, proponents of civil rights are extremely troubled by the measure since there is an associated risk with the vast expansion of government authority; their main worry is that law enforcement authorities will abuse these extraordinary powers.

These concerns about the extent of government influence are the focus of this work. More specifically, this book develops a comprehensive understanding of the relationship between the law and police behavior. Never in our history has such an understanding been so consequential. As we shall see, the police powers that are legislated to fight terrorism and, in general, crime can become so expanded that they could destroy the very freedoms that democratic society stands for. This book will articulate and study those issues which could threaten freedom. It will develop a theoretical foundation to explain these weighty issues in practical terms—questions such as, are professionally trained police officers likely to abuse their legal authority? If so, in what types of situations will this abuse occur? Is there a method to draft legislation so that it will be more effective at giving the police power yet, at the same time, properly restrain law enforcement?

PUBLIC INTERACTIONS WITH POLICE

Some may feel that these legal issues with respect to police do not personally affect them. Yet, it is unquestionable that they have the potential to touch every person. Think carefully about the following situations that could involve you. It is ten o'clock on a warm summer night in a crime-ridden neighborhood. You are walking down a deserted street, returning from work. Two people swiftly and unexpectedly jump out of a four-door car screeching to a halt beside you. You notice they have guns! Fearing for your life, you begin to run. They emphatically scream directly at you, "Police, don't move!" You then see what appear to be police shields dangling from chains around their necks. You are visibly shaking.

You decide your best course of action—since they have guns and claim to be police—is to stop and submit to them. Every second you are asking yourself, "Are these two police officers or criminals?" You are hoping this will end soon. Sweat is pouring down your face. You fear the worst. Soon they frisk you, apparently looking for a weapon. After frisking you, they search your pants pocket and remove a pen. Then one of them asks your name and why you are in the area. You are nervous and manage to give them your identification and tell them that you are returning from work. After verifying your name, using what appears to be a police radio, they return your pen and identification, then tell you that you fit the description of a robbery suspect. They apologize and allow you to leave. You feel unsure, scared, and even violated. Apparently, they were plainclothes police officers. You finally calm down and wonder—perhaps a bit angrily—can the police legally do this to me? Did these officers violate my constitutional rights?

These are typical responses to a police encounter—fear, and sometimes anger. Even the most innocuous of police interactions with the public cause people to feel nervous. Indeed, most of us can recall, for example, a feeling of intense anxiety associated with seeing a police car, its turret lights on, in our rearview mirror. Possibly the police car was not trying to stop you. In that case, you heaved a sigh of relief. If the police were stopping you, uh-oh, look out! You were likely very nervous.

Perhaps you can recall a time when you were taking an airplane from a foreign country. I remember a flight I took from London to New York. I was frisked and had my bags checked several times. Just before entering the gate to my flight, I was searched again. This time the authorities used a laptop computer. They rubbed what appeared to be a cotton swab over my carry-on bag to determine if there was any explosive material on it. My wife was quite angry at this point. Nevertheless, they conducted the search—ultimately finding nothing suspicious. Even though I am a trained New York City police officer with twenty years' experience who understands the need for such intrusions, and am aware of the requirements of the law, the situation still made me feel uncomfortable.

Such interactions between law enforcement and the public are commonplace. There is, therefore, a need to improve our understanding of these typical interactions. Subsequent chapters will explain many of these interactions and the importance of legal issues with respect to American policing. My aim is to improve our understanding of many thought-provoking theoretical issues at the center of our culture and democracy.

UNDERSTANDING THE LAW

In order to study the influence of the law on police, it is necessary to understand key terms. The law that will be closely scrutinized here is authoritative, decisional law which is based on constitutional or statutory interpretation and application. This would especially involve procedural law, as interpreted by local, state, and federal courts, and contained in the United States Constitution, in state constitutions, and in laws such as the New York State Criminal Procedure Law. What is the procedural law?

Criminal Law and the Law of Criminal Procedure

Police in the United States have the responsibility of enforcing criminal laws. Criminal laws—burglary, larceny, robbery, rape, and so on—are familiar to most people. If someone forcibly steals the property of another using a gun, the police are tasked with arresting that person for violating the criminal law—in this case, committing robbery. Likewise, if someone forces another to have sexual intercourse without the other's permission, that person has committed rape. The police can and will arrest the perpetrators of such crimes. Thus, police in American society are empowered to enforce the criminal law.

The powers of police to enforce the criminal laws are explicated in what is called the law of criminal procedure (e.g., New York State Criminal Procedure Law). In the law of criminal procedure, the powers that police officers have and the circumstances in which it is permissible for officers to use that power are written. Under the appropriate circumstances, police can, for example, legally stop, question, search, arrest, and use force—including deadly force. However, these powers are not endless. There are important limitations on the powers of police under the law of criminal procedure. For example, the police cannot simply arrest anyone they choose—they must have some proof that the person they intend to arrest did the crime. (The level of proof necessary is termed "probable cause.") Also, they cannot stop everyone on the street in order to find a perpetrator—they must have some proof, but not as much as that needed for arrest, to stop a suspect. (This level of proof necessary is called "reasonable suspicion.")

My focus is on the law of criminal procedure. Criminal procedure law (as opposed to criminal law) is founded on certain principles crucial to our government. In particular, the Bill of Rights (the first ten amendments to the Constitution) is one of the cornerstones of the procedure law. For example, the Fourth Amendment protects people from unreasonable searches and seizures; the Fifth Amendment, among other protections, safeguards people from self-incrimination.

The procedure law can be quite complicated because it is based on laws and rules that are constantly being interpreted and reinterpreted by the judiciary. One of the most familiar cases in this area is *Miranda v. Arizona* (1966). This United States Supreme Court case basically held that police must read suspects their rights before questioning them in police custody (i.e., "You have the right to remain silent, . . ."). This case gave a new rule for police to follow—read a person in police custody his or her constitutional rights before questioning.[1] Police must, therefore, be rigorously trained in the law such that they are familiarized with many legal criteria necessary to lawfully use their authorized powers. However, because this area of the law is very complicated (as will be discussed), the procedural law is very difficult to put into practice.

As a police officer and supervisor in the field, I have been involved in countless incidents requiring a need for knowledge of the law. One incident in particular stands out. At the time of this incident I had been a police officer for four years. I was working with a new officer who had recently graduated from the Police Academy. We were on routine patrol when an individual flagged down our marked radio car. The person who stopped us complained that the man on the corner had burglarized his apartment four days earlier. I inquired how he knew this. The man replied, "Because I have been suspicious of him for a long time now." The complainant had nothing else—no evidence whatsoever, just a hunch. My partner started to get out of the radio car and stated, "I am going to make an arrest." Recall that some evidence, called "probable cause," is necessary to make an arrest. Before he left the vehicle, I said, "You can't do that just yet, you don't have probable cause." My partner then asked, "What's probable cause?"

Needless to say, the arrest was not made. After I explained that you cannot make an arrest without probable cause (see especially *Watson v. United States* [1976]), I realized that he did know he needed some evidence (i.e., probable cause) but never understood the ramifications of this until presented with a situation requiring its use. We were constrained by the law and did not make the arrest. Had we made the arrest, I am sure that any number of supervisors, who verify arrests, would have caught the error. In this instance, we see how superficial knowledge was not being applied properly to a street situation. This real-life scenario aptly demonstrates the importance of studying this topic. In this case, the law did influence us. However, does it influence others?

Exclusionary Rule

One remedy for police violations of the procedure law is called the exclusionary rule. The exclusionary rule, simply stated, prevents illegally obtained evidence from being used in court proceedings against a defendant. For example, if police get a confession or seize property without following established legal procedures (e.g., not reading a suspect his/

her *Miranda* rights), that evidence cannot be used against the defendant during court proceedings. It is not unusual for hearings to take place—prior to trial—to determine whether or not the evidence can be admitted by the prosecution. It is often stated that this judicially created remedy is aimed at influencing law enforcement's behavior. However, other reasons have been cited.

Two basic reasons for the exclusionary rule are described by Oaks (1970). He describes the normative and factual explanations. The normative justification, sometimes called the *judicial integrity rationale*, states that the rule is needed to prevent the judiciary from being a "party to lawless invasions" (Oaks, 1970: 669). That is, the rule prevents the judiciary from appearing to conspire with the police in collecting illegally obtained evidence. The factual justification, or *deterrence rationale*, suggests that excluding evidence will reduce violations of search and seizure rules by law enforcement. The exclusionary rule's long history further helps to shed light on its purpose.

The roots of the exclusionary rule are contained in the United States Supreme Court case *Weeks v. United States* (1914).[2] In this case, federal law enforcement officers were ordered by the Court to abide by the exclusionary rule. However, from 1914 through the mid-1950s the *silver platter doctrine* was in effect. This doctrine involved two ways of circumventing the exclusionary rule from *Weeks*. First, evidence could still be illegally obtained by state officers and then given to the federal authorities. This practice was terminated by the *Elkins rule* (*Elkins v. United States* [1960]). The second situation was one in which federal agents would engage in illegal activity and then turn over the evidence to the states. This practice ended with *Rea v. United States* (1956). However, since these Supreme Court decisions were aimed at federal law enforcement, it was still possible for state and local authorities to conduct an illegal search and have the evidence admitted in state courts. That is, some states did not have an exclusionary rule.

This situation was challenged in *Wolf v. Colorado* (1949). In this case, the United States Supreme Court basically held that in a conviction in a state court for a state offense, the Fourteenth Amendment does *not* forbid the admission of evidence obtained by an unreasonable search and seizure.[3] The Court declined to apply the *Weeks* exclusionary rule to the states. However, the Court in *Wolf v. Colorado* also wrote that "such a police incursion into privacy . . . would run counter to the guaranty of the Fourteenth Amendment." The Fourteenth Amendment was passed right after the Civil War, during Reconstruction. The equal protection clause in the Fourteenth Amendment forbids states to pass legislation that denies any person equal protection of the laws. This clause has generally been interpreted broadly by the courts to justify giving many basic rights to people. Thus, the Court in *Wolf* did *absorb* the Fourth Amendment into the Fourteenth Amendment and apply it to the states. However, the remedy of the exclusionary rule was not yet applied. States were free to choose the remedy, and some did not utilize an exclusionary rule.

It was not until 1961, in *Mapp v. Ohio,* that the United States Supreme Court applied the exclusionary rule to the states. Today, case law is replete with examples of the Supreme Court and other courts attempting to explain and limit police power. The Fourth Amendment line of cases is particularly striking. For example, *California v. Greenwood* (1988) [no reasonable expectation for privacy of garbage at the curb]; *Oliver v. United States* (1984) [open fields doctrine—land around and associated with a house is resolved by several factors, but the key is a reasonable expectation of privacy]; *Katz v. United States* (1967) [the government made an illegal search and seizure by listening in on telephone calls made from a telephone booth even though the government did not physically enter the booth; the key to deciding "what is an illegal search and seizure" is determining "what is a reasonable expectation of privacy"]. Thousands of other cases could be cited here. Some might explain what a search is (e.g., *United States v. Place* [1983] explains the canine sniff is not a search)[4]; others explain what a seizure is (e.g., *Andresen v. Maryland* [1976] explains that basically anything related to evidence may be seized). Many cases involve spelling out the exceptions to a search warrant, such as a search incident to a lawful arrest, an officer seeing evidence or contraband in plain view, people giving consent to the officer, an emergency that exists where the officer must immediately enter, and so on.

The point is that written law, which is explained by the courts, is obviously aimed at restricting police power. That is, theoretically, the police are constrained by all these rules. Furthermore, we can see that these cases are fairly recent, bringing up questions about the ability of police to properly follow newly decided judicial rulings (judicial impact theory).

RECENT CHANGES IN THE LEGAL LANDSCAPE

The "due process revolution," which took place from about the late 1950s to the early 1970s, has radically altered the legal landscape for police officers (Israel and LaFave, 1988). It has been suggested that during this period many officers began to realize the limits on their authority, especially those of the Fourth and Fifth Amendments. In particular, court cases such as *Mapp v. Ohio* (1961) and *Miranda v. Arizona* (1966) struck the policing profession like a bolt of lightning. Or did they?

Some anecdotal evidence suggests that radical changes took place after these decisions. For example, Kamisar (1979: 349) asks, "Why did the police have to make such strenuous efforts to comply with *Mapp* unless they had not been complying with the Fourth Amendment?" Leonard Reisman, former Deputy Commissioner of the New York City Police Department, is quoted as saying, "Before this [*Mapp*] nobody bothered to take out search warrants" (Kamisar, 1979: 349). In a Columbia Law School study a high-ranking official in the Narcotics Bureau of the New York City Police Department stated, "Before *Mapp* there was nothing to restrain enforcement. Anything was legal" (Columbia Law School, 1986: 94). Thus, professional police administrators in the 1960s apparently were scrambling to overhaul their departments.

My recent informal discussion with officers who graduated the New York City Police Academy during the 1960s (the Academy is considered one of the nation's most advanced law enforcement training facilities) clearly indicates that legal training at the time was minimal, at best. Furthermore, those training standards were, simply put, far above the accepted norm of that era. This suggests that much of the research conducted in the 1960s and 1970s which examines the impact of decisions like *Miranda* and *Mapp* may have missed the vast legal changes because much of the impact extends far into the future, perhaps even to today. This is because it takes time for a court decision to markedly influence the behavior of street-level crime-fighting practitioners. After a court case is decided, it takes time to communicate it, and training and other such matters must be addressed before behavioral changes occur. Hardened street officers are not likely to display an overwhelming behavioral swing of the magnitude that cases such as *Mapp* and *Miranda* call for after merely being told of the decision (assuming they were informed). To cause such a paradigm shift, it would likely take a great deal of time and effort. As Canon (1979: 402) states, "Experience tells us that sudden and dramatic changes in policy such as occurred with the *Mapp* decision do not produce alteration in behavior overnight."

Officers *today* are much more extensively trained in the powers that they legally possess. Local, state, and federal legal guidelines are covered in detail in most Police Academy curricula, including New York City (see Purpura, 1997: 180–181; Schmalleger, 1995: 225–227).[5] Additionally, there are many training sessions for officers working in the field. This is a radical departure from the days when an officer had little or no formal instruction.

Also, numerous safeguards and controls have been introduced or strengthened specifically to better enforce the legal limitations that restrict the power of law enforcement officers. In New York City these include an all-civilian-staffed Civilian Complaint Review Board, internal affairs units, field internal affairs units, inspections units, integrity control officers in each precinct, the increased threat of civil suits, local and federal district attorneys specifically assigned to "police the police," and special commissions designed to study and root out all aspects of corruption (e.g., the Mollen Commission in New York City).

Although it is unusual, officers must also be cognizant of the possibility of arrest for conducting an illegal search and seizure. Lieutenant Patricia Feerick of the New York City Police Department, for example, was arrested for conducting an illegal search. It should be noted that Lieutenant Feerick is also a lawyer. She claimed that the loss of a police radio was an emergency exception to the need for a warrant (see *People v. Love* [1994] and *People v. Mitchell* [1976]). Her assertions were denied by the court. This case demonstrates the possibility of police officers being arrested for conducting an illegal search. Importantly, arrest is usually not cited by legal and policing experts as a possible consequence of conducting an illegal search. Experts routinely suggest that civil suits and exclusion are the remedies for conducting an illegal search (see, e.g., Kamisar, 1979; Canon, 1979; Davies, 1983; Heffernan, 1989; Heffernan and Lovely, 1991; Loewenthal, 1980).

Recent changes in the legal landscape, then, suggest the need for further legal study. This is especially true because, as stated previously, it takes time for court decisions to filter down to street-level practitioners. This process not only involves communicating the decisions to officers but also explaining specifically how their behavior is, or should be, affected (e.g., training issues). Given continuing police professionalization with internal impetus, external pressures for accountability, and concern about civil liability, it seems likely that laws will have more influence on police behavior. Additionally, it is possible, and even probable, that a whole generation of law enforcement officers needed to retire before these legal changes could have a substantial impact.

Officers who work the streets or who are only minimally trained in legal issues may be resistant to such legal changes of the kind we are discussing. It seems likely that the due process revolution may, in fact, have much more impact today, years later, after administrators, supervisors, and officers who were trained in the 1960s and 1970s leave the policing profession. Additionally, there are many other issues closely related to the topic under investigation that will, it is hoped, lead to more lawful policing techniques.

NEW YORK STATE COURT OF APPEALS

The New York State Court of Appeals has been described as undermining the decisions of the United States Supreme Court with respect to decisions affecting police behavior (i.e., procedure law). Recent periodical literature, for example, has blasted the New York State courts on this issue. Reinharz (1996: 45–46), writing for the *City Journal*, specifically discusses New York's Court of Appeals; he states, "Street encounters between police and suspects is a prime area in which the Court of Appeals has swept aside the commonsense judgment of cops and erected instead an absurd, hopelessly confusing framework of legal rules." The state courts have done this by granting more rights under state constitutions. A case that exemplifies this is *United States v. Leon* (1984).

In *Leon* the Supreme Court adopted the "good faith exception." If the police act with a reasonable reliance on a search warrant issued by a detached and neutral magistrate, then (even upon the ultimate finding that the search warrant lacked probable cause) as long as the officers acted with an "objectively reasonable belief" that the search warrant was valid, the evidence will not be excluded. In New York State, for example, the good faith exception to the search warrant requirement does not apply as per *People v. Bigelow* (1985).[6] Additionally, the Court of Appeals has been questioned for its lack of clarity. The Governor of New York State, George Pataki, and other commentators and academics have stated that the Court of Appeals in New York (and other courts as well) is exceedingly unclear (to put it mildly) in its jurisprudence (see, e.g., Rothwax, 1996).

THE IMPORTANCE OF THE NEW YORK CITY
POLICE DEPARTMENT

The New York City Police Department (NYPD) has been the focal point of controversial arguments on legal issues and police. My work as a police captain and sworn officer with the NYPD for over twenty years will help develop this understanding. In this section, I will explain why the NYPD is so important to understanding the law and police behavior.

Myriad turbulent controversies regarding the law and policing are occurring in New York City. Many of these legal controversies emanate from alleged police abuse of authority, especially with respect to search and seizure and stop and frisk practices by police. Public outcry against these alleged abuses, especially from minority communities, has been nearly universal. Incidents in New York City, such as the sexual abuse of a Haitian immigrant, Abner Louima, by police and two separate shootings of unarmed black men by police (Amadou Diallo and Patrick Dorismond), fuel the fires of tension.

With respect to these incidents, the legal practices of the NYPD have been, and continue to be, under intense scrutiny. Criminologists, police practitioners, lawyers, politicians, and others are engaged in widespread debate about legal issues in policing; the debate involves political figures such as former Mayor Rudolph Giuliani, Governor George Pataki, Attorney General Eliot Spitzer, and community activist Reverend Al Sharpton; academics including George Kelling, Jeffrey Fagan, and Eli Silverman; police managers such as former New York City Police Commissioners William Bratton and Howard Safir; and many others. Some take the position that the police are to be commended; others believe the police should be criticized for their behaviors.

Rationale for Studying NYPD Legal Behavior

Why are New York City police the subject of enormous scrutiny regarding their legal behavior? One reason is that legal policing issues have come to the forefront of the national agenda. With the terrorist attacks of September 11, the O.J. Simpson trial of the 1990s, recent community unrest, and racial profiling, issues involving many police agencies in the United States have received national and international attention. Admitted racial profiling by New Jersey State Troopers certainly raised eyebrows about police legal behavior, especially in minority communities. Another cause for concern is that one of the flagship police departments in the United States, the Los Angeles Police Department, has been placed under a consent decree (a legally binding agreement between disputing parties that, in the case of a police department, forces that department to work under various restrictions with the court's authority overseeing those restrictions, such as recording and reporting stops) for many of these legal issues, including vehicle and pedestrian stops, with the Department of Justice. Works such as Skolnick and Fyfe's *Above the Law* (1993), Dershowitz's (1996) *Reasonable Doubts*, and Rothwax's *Guilty: The Collapse of Criminal Justice* (1996) also contributed to concern about police and legal issues. Today, nearly everyone is familiar with "racial profiling," "illegal search," and "*Miranda* rights."

Government Investigations into the Legal Practices of the NYPD

Enormous amounts of taxpayer dollars have been spent investigating the NYPD's legal practices on the street. New York State Attorney General Eliot Spitzer, for example, conducted a large-scale project regarding the stop practices of the NYPD. On December 1, 1999, he officially released

a scathing report on the practices of the NYPD with regard to racial profiling. The emphasis of the report was on a quantitative analysis conducted
by Professor Jeffrey Fagan of Columbia University.

Dr. Fagan statistically analyzed Stop and Frisk Reports prepared by
New York City police officers from January 1, 1998, through March 31,
1999 (supplied by the NYPD). The critical findings from this report were
the following: "There is a strong statistical correlation between race and
likelihood of being stopped. While crime rates partially explain the high
correlation between race and likelihood of being 'stopped,' they do not
fully explain this correlation. . . . In roughly one out of every seven 'stops'
conducted by the NYPD, the facts that the police officer articulates for
making the 'stop,'. . . fail to meet the legal threshold of 'reasonable suspicion'" (Attorney General, 1999: 89). Dr. Fagan is strongly suggesting that the police in New York City often conduct illegal stops on the
basis of a person's race. Interestingly, the Attorney General's report also
found that "the law's guideposts are clear enough" with respect to stop
and frisk.

These findings are extremely controversial. The NYPD vociferously
responded to the Attorney General's report. On November 30, 1999,
Police Commissioner Howard Safir stated in a press release, "It is most
unfortunate that the Attorney General sees the publication of this critically flawed report as the proper starting point for a dialogue between
his office and the NYPD."[7] He continued, "The race of the individuals
stopped strongly correlates with the descriptions of persons committing
violent crime as identified by their victims." Commissioner Safir was arguing that the disparity in stops (by race) is due to whom victims identify as perpetrators. Thus, though police admittedly stop more minorities,
the NYPD argues this has nothing to do with discrimination (i.e., racial
profiling). Police are merely legally stopping those people who fit descriptions given by victims of crime.

Another weakness of the Attorney General's report is that it assumes
that Stop and Frisk Reports prepared by police officers document legal
justifications for stops. In its press release the NYPD argued, "Stop and
frisk forms are administrative documents, and are not meant to be used
as conclusive evidence of an underlying legal basis for a stop." Compounding the aforementioned issues, the Attorney General's report also claimed
that the law is clear in this area (Attorney General, 1999: 29–30). The
vast majority of commentators and experts vehemently differ with the
Attorney General's assessment of the current condition of the law with
respect to policing—especially in New York State. Countless experts,
including the Governor of New York (see, e.g., "The Governor's
Attack . . . ," 1996), have been especially critical of the courts for their

lack of clarity in this area (other examples include Goldstein, 1992; Rothwax, 1996; Israel and LaFave, 1988; Amsterdam, 1974; Reinharz, 1996; and Baum, 1985).

The NYPD, however, is not alone in its criticism of the Attorney General's report. For example, a recent study authored by Engel, Calnon, and Bernard (2002) is extremely critical of all the current research on racial profiling to date (including the Attorney General's Report). Similar to NYPD's argument, they emphatically state, "the literature on racial profiling is misleading, fails to include crucial explanatory variables, and provides a limited understanding of the phenomenon. Accordingly, no firm policy implications can be derived from this research" (Shepard, Engel, Calnon, Bernard, 2002: 249–274).

The United States Civil Rights Commission also was very disapproving of the NYPD's legal practices. With regard to the stop and frisk behavior, the Commission reiterated many of the points in the Attorney General's report. Other than narrative accounts from various interviews, the Civil Rights Commission appears to have accomplished very little new research. Thus, it did little to add to the state of knowledge on this issue. This left the Commission open to strong criticism by the NYPD. In fact, the NYPD response to the Commission's report was scathing. With great fanfare and publicity, in May 2000 Police Commissioner Howard Safir unveiled a lengthy response that essentially undercut the Commission's report: "The overall methodology of the Draft Report of the U.S. Commission on Civil Rights Report recklessly relies almost exclusively on unsupported and uninvestigated anecdotal allegations or statements made by individuals, organizations, or media sources without independent verification or fact finding performed by the Commission. Where facts are offered by Mayor Giuliani or Police Commissioner Safir, they are consistently and expressly doubted in the Report" (NYCPD "Response to the Draft Report of the United States Commission on Civil Rights—Police Practices and Civil Rights in New York City," 2000: 1).

Another government agency, the New York City Civilian Complaint Review Board (CCRB), reviews NYPD's legal activity. The CCRB describes itself as "an independent, non-police city agency with the authority to investigate allegations of police misconduct filed by members of the public against New York City police officers. The Board receives, investigates, makes findings, and recommends discipline to the Police Commissioner on complaints alleging Force, Abuse of Authority, Discourtesy and Offensive Language" (CCRB web site, www.nyc.gov/html/ccrb/home.html).

The CCRB released a report on stop and frisk practices of the NYPD in June 2001. They examined civilian complaints related to street stops that were closed between January 1, 1997, and March 31, 1999.[8] There were 1,346 closed cases that the CCRB focused on. However, at the beginning of its report, it acknowledged that over 250,000 stops by the NYPD occurred during this time period. This means that the NYPD had very few complaints (i.e., 54 complaints for every 10,000 stops). This, of course, strengthens the NYPD's case that stop behavior by its officers is, for the most part, legal.

The CCRB's key findings also were not much of a surprise. For example, they found that African Americans and men are more likely to make civilian complaints about stops (CCRB, 2001: 4). This finding fits neatly with the NYPD argument that officers are stopping those people identified by victims as committing violent crime who are predominantly African American and male. Thus, we expect, simply due to the greater proportion of African Americans and men being stopped, that these two groups will make civilian complaints more often because they are more likely to be identified as perpetrators by victims (as seen on NYPD complaint reports) and are therefore apt to be stopped. Further, since stops generally deal with completely innocent people who, for example, by happenstance fit the description of someone who committed a crime, we expect a higher level of complaints. That is, the nature of stops are such that innocent people are often involved, which will likely lead to increased civilian complaints because they have done nothing wrong. This is unlike other police conduct, such as arrests and summonses, where the person is more likely to have committed an illegal act (partially because a higher level of proof is required). Last, the CCRB report's recommendations were, for the most part, adopted by the NYPD before the report was released. For example, the CCRB recommends that police officers "offer a reason for the stop" (CCRB, 2001: 6). Police Commissioner Bernard B. Kerik had already adopted, on January 1, 2001, new procedures and a new form that incorporated this recommendation. Nevertheless, the CCRB Report was yet another government report with a negative assessment of the NYPD's legal practices in this area.

Compstat and "Broken Windows" Theory

Another important reason that the NYPD is under such intense scrutiny is that the New York City area has seen an astounding decrease in crime.[9] According to NYPD statistics (which are supplied to the Federal Bureau of Investigation for the Uniform Crime Reports), New York City saw a drop in crime every year from 1992 through 2000.[10] The most precipitous drops occurred in 1995 (−16.1 percent) and 1996 (−14 percent).[11] In fact, this huge decrease was responsible for much of the entire nation's decrease in crime during the same period.

Experts in policing differ as to the explanations for this decrease. William Bratton, the New York City Police Commissioner in 1994 and 1995, debated with criminologists over this issue. In Boston, at the American Society of Criminology meeting on November 18, 1995, Commissioner Bratton was involved in a debate with leading criminologists over whether the Police Department was responsible for the decrease in crime. The criminologists left the debate basically feeling that more study was needed to determine why crime was dropping and they expressed doubts that other phenomena (e.g., economics, less use of crack cocaine) were not also contributing to the drop (see Krauss, 1995a; Bratton, 1996). More recently, the same debate has surfaced again. For example, Robert Gangi (1997), who sides with the criminologists, and Eli Silverman (1997), who feels the Police Department should be given more credit, published newspaper articles in a public debate on the issue.

Silverman and Bratton, among others, argue that management at the NYPD was, at least partially, responsible for the drop in crime. One well-known tool used by management, which is claimed to have helped reduce crime in the NYPD, is the process called Compstat. Compstat meetings are held twice a week from seven to ten in the morning, normally on Wednesdays and Fridays (these early times supposedly prevent conflict with other meetings). Commanding Officers (C.O.'s) have been transferred and/or had other disciplinary action taken against them due to poor performance at Compstat. This discipline is often meted out for failing to address precinct conditions, especially increases in crime statistics.

Compstat attempts to control police behavior by focusing, to a great extent, on the power of higher-ranking officers and, in particular, the C.O. of a precinct.[12] Compstat meetings involve very high-ranking officers holding the C.O. accountable for everything that occurs in the precinct, including especially, but not exclusively, crime statistics. Thus, pressures on C.O.'s at Compstat are varied but focus on reducing crime. This often means putting pressure on precinct police officers to make arrests and reduce crime. As part of the Compstat process, the steps to reduce crime to be taken by C.O.'s are described by the police department as accurate and timely intelligence, rapid deployment, effective tactics, and relentless follow-up and assessment (Andrews, 1995).

The NYPD's model of policing (including Compstat) is most closely associated with the Broken Windows Theory espoused by Professor George Kelling. Kelling had an important role in the development of the NYPD model. He worked closely with Police Commissioner Bratton both at the NYPD and when Bratton was in charge of the New York City Transit Police (when the latter was a separate agency in the early 1990s). As Kelling (1999: 1) writes, "Police activities to restore public order in New York City and its subway system, for instance, have received extensive publicity and attention. So, too, has the 'broken windows' metaphor as it has been closely linked to New York City." Essentially this theory emphasizes that in order to attack all crimes, even serious ones, there is a need to focus on even trivial violations (e.g., graffiti, panhandlers, etc.) For example, Kelling and Catherine Coles in their book *Fixing Broken Windows: Restoring Order and Reducing Crime in Our Communities* suggest, "When it comes to index crimes such as homicide, there is growing evidence to suggest that police attention to 'quality-of-life' issues and low-level crimes, making use of tactics significantly at variance with low-level crimes, making use of tactics significantly at variance with 911 policing, may have a significant impact in lowering incidence rates of index crimes" (Kelling and Coles, 1996: 100). Consequently, understanding the overall effects of the model of policing in New York City is important both to practitioners and to those interested in studying theory.

One issue that needs to be examined closely is whether a reduction in crime is purchased at the price of an increase in illegal police abuse. This question is especially important because the Compstat process has received numerous accolades from police administrators and academicians alike (see Silverman, 1997). Its success has been considered tantamount to an upheaval in policing administration. Numerous police agencies are attempting to replicate the process in their jurisdictions (see especially Silverman, 1999).

Crime Control Versus Due Process Models

Herbert Packer in his discourse on the courts and the police points out that "the kind of criminal process that we have is profoundly affected by a series of competing value choices which, consciously or unconsciously, serve to resolve tensions that arise in the system." He subsequently describes two models of criminal justice programs to which he ascribes different values. First, he outlines the *Crime Control Model* as "the efficient, expeditious and reliable screening and disposition of persons suspected of crime as the central value to be served by the criminal process." The other model he calls the *Due Process model*. Packer explains that this model "sees that function [the criminal process] as limited by, and subordinate to, the maintenance of the dignity and autonomy of the individual." Packer points out that these models are "polar extremes which, in real life, are subject to almost infinite modulation" (Packer, 1966: 238–239).

This dichotomy of crime control versus due process provides a useful framework for discussion. In today's world of law enforcement, crime control strategies are plentiful. For example, the emphasis of Compstat in New York City is on reducing crime. Similar strategies by law enforcement abound with the rhetoric of reducing crime. One has only to pick up a newspaper to read about quality of life crackdowns for, say, "road rage" or "driving while intoxicated." The ultimate goal of such crackdowns is reducing crime. As the NYPD states, "The success of this strategic control system and our Crime Control and Quality of Life Strategies are evidenced by the tremendous declines in crime we have achieved since 1993" (New York City Police Department, 1998: 1). Policing strategies, then, tend to focus on decreasing crime, and have been praised by some as having a significant impact on the number of reported offenses (see especially Bratton, 1996; Silverman, 1997; Kelling and Coles, 1996).

Reducing crime is a worthy goal, but along with decreases in crime may come other, less desirable consequences. An understanding of Packer's dichotomy is helpful in identifying possible areas of difficulty that an agency focusing on crime control might have. Since many programs initiated by today's police managers are basically targeted at *crime control*, it seems reasonable to hypothesize that if such programs are not carefully implemented, *due process* considerations are likely to suffer. That is, as more emphasis is placed on crime control, there is increased stress on due process.

If we assume the above hypothesis to be true, then an intense focus on crime control may ultimately lead to a decline in the values of police officers associated with the due process model. More specifically, in a crime control environment, the pressure on police officers of every rank is to reduce the number of reported crimes. This pressure may ultimately manifest itself as overzealous enforcement behavior. That is, some officers could be reacting to the unyielding stress to reduce crime by abusing their authority (e.g., conducting illegal searches, stops, arrests).

This abuse of authority is the antithesis of policing in a democracy. As stated, values such as high integrity, the importance of protecting every human life, and respecting the dignity of each individual are critical to democratic policing. There is cause for concern when we empower the police without a counterbalance.[13]

Academics and others have recognized this dilemma for the police. For example, Herman Goldstein suggests that in some departments the concern for crime control overwhelms due process considerations. Goldstein (1977: 13) writes:

> The police are not only obligated to exercise their limited authority in conformity with the Constitution and legislatively enacted restrictions; they are

obligated as well to see to it that others do not infringe on constitutionally guaranteed rights. These requirements introduce into the police function the unique dimension that makes policing in this country such a high calling. One of the consequences of the current situation is that the police in some communities, especially in the congested areas of large cities, place a higher priority on maintaining order than on operating legally.

Even Kelling and Coles (1996: 163, 168–169), staunch proponents of aggressive crime control policing, recognize the possible consequences of empowering police to fight crime:

Whether explicitly or not, libertarians understand that the shift toward community policing, with the accompanying commitment to order maintenance and problem solving, represents a movement toward a far more aggressive and interventionist police strategy . . . individual rights are on the line when police engage in order maintenance. . . . The authority accorded police by law and the mandate from the community under which they operate does not constitute a license for them to violate individual rights.

Relevant Statistics and Comments by Academics

Recent civilian complaint statistics seem to suggest that there may have been a problem with officers abusing their authority in New York City (see Table 1.1). Note that 1995 and 1996 are the years of the greatest decrease in crime and have the greatest increases in civilian complaints for abuse of authority.[14]

Two newspaper articles, from different papers within the city, discuss this issue. Krauss wrote in the *New York Times* (1996: B1):

There are three key elements of Mr. Bratton's approach: a relentless focus on attacking so-called quality-of-life offenses as a way to combat more serious crimes; a thorough overhaul of personnel, strategies and training within the department, and dollops of symbolism and bravado. . . . [How-

Table 1.1
Allegations of Abuse of Authority (Primary Allegations): Civilian Complaints

Year	1993	1994	1995	1996	1997	1998	1999	2000
Complaints	1,236	2,027	2,560	3,113	2,788	3,156	3,038	2,319

Source: Civilian Complaint Review Board, Status Report January–December 2000, p. 35.

ever] while the department under Mr. Bratton increased arrests by 25 percent, there was an increase of more than 50 percent in civilian complaints about police misconduct and brutality in the minority communities where the drops in violent crime were sharpest. Moreover, the department weathered two major precinct corruption scandals, in which more than 50 officers were charged with crimes ranging from drug dealing to perjury.

Rashbaum (1996) similarly wrote in the *New York Daily News*: "Civilian complaints against police for allegedly illegal searches skyrocketed by 135% in the first two years of Mayor Giuliani's 'quality of life' crackdown."

Increases in the number of court claims for abuse by officers, as well as payments for civil suits against police, further indicate that abuse of authority in the NYPD was, at a minimum, troublesome. Purdy (1997: A1) writes, "From 1994 to 1996, the city received 8,316 court claims of abuse by officers, compared with 5,983 for the three previous years." In fiscal year 1995 the city paid $19.5 million in settlements for police misconduct (Sontag and Barry, 1997; Rohde, 1998). Comparing that figure with the 1996 figure of $27.3 million certainly suggests that there was a problem of systemic abuse of authority in the police department (Sontag and Barry, 1997). Other jurisdictions are experiencing similar problems. Los Angeles, for example, spent $20 million on civil suits in 1992 (Rayner, 1995). And other studies suggest that awards are higher than in the past (Meadows and Trostle, 1988; McCoy, 1985). One reason for these facts could be the intense focus by the New York City Police and other police departments on crime control.

Academics, too, have suggested that a focus on crime can create legal concerns for police. The study of New York City officers by Loewenthal (1980), for example, suggests that police are deterred when the law is clear but that the demands of ranking officers to make arrests and possibly violate the law are very strong. Loewenthal (1980: 32–35) states:

Spurred by pressures for arrests from their commanders, police investigators are often tempted to violate the warrant and probable cause requirements of the fourth amendment in order to obtain enough evidence to substantiate a sufficient number of arrests. However, many police officers are apparently deterred from searches that are clearly illegal because of the problem created by the exclusionary rule.

More recently, Dershowitz (1996), citing official reports, suggests that supervisors (especially commanding officers) are encouraging illegal searches in New York City. He discusses the results of the Mollen

Commission (an official commission set up by New York City to study corruption in the NYPD). Quoting the Mollen Commission Dershowitz (1996: 52) states, "The practice of police falsification in connection with such arrests is so common in certain precincts that it has spawned its own word: 'testilying.' . . . Even more troubling . . . the evidence suggests that the . . . commanding officer not only tolerated but encouraged, this unlawful practice."

SUMMARY

Recent events such as the terrorist attacks in New York City have brought to the forefront concerns about the extent of government power with respect to enforcing the law. The issues involved with this affect each of us. The focus of this book is on studying the law of criminal procedure, the permissible powers that government officials have to enforce criminal laws. The procedure law can be very complicated due to rules that are constantly being modified by the judiciary. The exclusionary rule is one important remedy aimed at preventing police abuse of power. Recent changes in the legal landscape, especially during the 1960s due process revolution, and changes in police training have made study of this issue even more timely and important. In particular, the NYPD has been the focal point of much debate and inquiry. There are many reasons for this: public outcry, especially following several well-publicized incidents of police abuse of authority; several independent government investigations that had unfavorable results for the NYPD; legal issues coming to the forefront of the national agenda; exceedingly large decreases in crime that may be due (at least in part) to police aggressiveness; increases in civilian complaints (especially for abuse of authority); claims by some academics of illegal behavior by officers (or at least the strong possibility of it); and vast changes in the legal landscape since the 1960s that should now be influencing officer behavior.

NOTES

1. There are many exceptions to this basic rule from other cases.
2. However, the rule goes even further back, to *Boyd v. United States* (1886), although it was not applied to all federal law enforcement officers until *Weeks*.
3. The Fourteenth Amendment is used by the Supreme Court to make the Bill of Rights applicable to the states.
4. However, the New York State Court of Appeals in *People v. Dunn* (1990) ruled that the canine sniff is a search under New York law. For example, the use of drug-sniffing dogs in a public hallway, in an attempt to determine if illegal drugs are in an apartment, is illegal in New York unless the officers have at least reasonable suspicion.

5. Today, *every* state mandates a minimum amount of training for police recruits (see Schmalleger, 1995: 225).

6. Again, the importance for researchers to examine state and local law before designing a study cannot be overemphasized.

7. The NYPD had an advance copy of the report, which was officially released the next day.

8. These civilian complaints occurred mostly in 1997 and 1998, although the report acknowledges that the actual period is from 1990 to 1999.

9. Many other big cities in the United States have seen a decrease, but generally generally not nearly as dramatic as New York City's (see FBI's Uniform Crime Reports).

10. Data supplied by the New York City Police Department's Office of Management Analysis and Planning (OMAP).

11. Statistics indicate overall crime drop for the yearly periods. Actual totals are 530,121 index crimes for 1994; 444,758 index crimes for 1995; and 382,555 index crimes for 1996. Numbers supplied by OMAP.

12. Others also go to these meetings such as Housing Police Service Area C.O.'s, Transit District C.O.'s, and supervising detectives.

13. This is what our system of government is all about: checks and balances. The police, as members of the executive branch, should be properly checked by the other branches of government (i.e., the judiciary and the legislature).

14. From January 10, 1994, to April 14, 1996, William J. Bratton was the Police Commissioner. These years had the greatest focus on quality of life. Howard Safir, the next Police Commissioner, instituted the Courtesy, Professionalism and Respect program. Bernard Kerik was Police Commissioner from August 21, 2000, through December 31, 2001. The current Police Commissioner is Raymond W. Kelly.

CHAPTER 2

Studying Legal Issues and Policing

We need to develop logical and comprehensive explanations of police officers' decision-making processes regarding their legal authority. This is accomplished using modern research techniques as well as traditional methods: analyzing and reviewing real-life situations, analyses of scientifically designed questionnaires (self reports) and official data, using years of experience as a police officer and supervisor, and studying available literature. This chapter conveys important information about basic policing and legal concepts, as well as ways to properly investigate those concepts. To that end, explanations of specific court cases, descriptions of those factors which influence police behavior with respect to the law, and a concise explanation of how to measure these phenomena are discussed.[1]

To study police legal behavior, one must first carry out the extremely arduous task of collecting accurate information about the police and their practices with respect to the law. This is a difficult task due to, at a minimum, three factors. First, these activities (e.g., stops, searches) are, in general, hidden from intense public scrutiny. This is because searches and stops do not occur on a stage but are activities that are rarely viewed openly. Second, it is difficult to supervise these activities. Supervisory activities involve review of paperwork, the reputation of the officer, and perhaps some, albeit minimal, observation (e.g., at a radio run, both supervisors and officers may be present at the same time). Third, the nature and extent of the judiciary's influence on police is not well understood even by experienced and learned researchers (see, e.g., Johnson and Canon, 1984: 224). Therefore, a study on police and the law will require innovative research techniques.

A SCIENTIFICALLY DESIGNED QUESTIONNAIRE

One important way to study police legal behavior is through the use of a scientifically designed questionnaire. This helps to gather measurable criteria from a large, representative sample of officers in a reasonable time frame. To that end, a questionnaire specifically designed to study legal police behavior was administered to New York City police officers who worked in precincts from May through June 1997.

A key feature of this survey administration was anonymity for respondents. That is, the researcher cannot link the responses to the names of those who answered the survey. This method of administration is clearly preferable for studying legal issues and police due to certain benefits derived from anonymity. In particular, anonymity helps in achieving truthful responses rather than socially desirable answers (Babbie, 1989; Bradburn, 1983; Dillman, 1983).[2] Thus, anonymity is essential in addressing the sensitive issue of legal police behavior. Since the questionnaire requires honest responses to questions about how officers might behave in ambiguous and even illegal situations, it is necessary for respondents to feel secure. Babbie (1989: 475), for example, writes, "In one study of drug use among university students during the 1960s, I decided that I specifically did not want to know the identity of respondents. I felt that honestly assuring anonymity would increase the likelihood and accuracy of responses." Bradburn (1983: 298) states, "With sensitive questions or those associated with a high degree of social desirability, the more anonymous methods of administration appear to work somewhat better." Accordingly, I utilized a carefully designed questionnaire that takes advantage of newly developed methods combined with anonymous techniques.

Questionnaire: Factorial Survey

The questionnaire includes three parts. Each segment measures different aspects of police behavior. The first part of the questionnaire is based on what is called the factorial survey method (Rossi and Nock, 1982). The factorial survey approach is an innovative research design that measures respondents' decision-making as the parameters of the decision-making context change. Basically, this means that the survey allows measurement of the extent to which one factor (such as the law) influences officers' decisions, compared to other factors (such as the police culture). This method is based on a complex set of hypothetical situations known as vignettes. Officers are asked to respond to a set of vignettes as if they were responding to street situations.[3] By carefully examining responses, one can determine the extent to which the law, compared to other (i.e., extralegal) factors, influences officers' decision-making in various street situations (e.g., stopping and/or searching someone).

Properly constructing the survey instrument is a complex task. Most important, one must develop specific wording that allows measurement of key factors. For this book, both legal factors (the law) and extralegal factors (other than the law) are examined. Certain extralegal factors were chosen because, as we shall see, extensive research suggests their impact on police legal behavior. These extralegal influences include the police culture, the community, and the police bureaucracy. These extralegal influences will be explained first, and then the legal factors. The Appendix contains the exact wording for each factor.

The Community

"The community" refers to the nature of the neighborhood in which the officer works. This can be exceedingly complicated. To simplify the analysis, many authors point out that the wealth (or lack thereof) of a community is a key influence on officer behavior. Wilson (1977), for example, feels that the socioeconomic composition of the neighborhood is critical to explaining police behavior. He points out that there are many factors which influence police behavior, such as "the *socioeconomic composition of the community*, the law enforcement standards set, implicitly or explicitly, by the political systems, and the special interests and concerns of the police chief" (Wilson, 1977: 143; italics added).

Others, too, suggest officers' legal behavior will be influenced by the level of wealth in a community. A case in point is seen in Skolnick's (1966) observational study. One pertinent argument he makes is that the greatest impact of searching first and asking questions later (illegal search and seizure) will be felt most strongly in ghetto areas. Galliher (1971) states that the police are likely to react "oppressively" in poor neighborhoods. Specifically, "one might predict . . . that in heterogeneous communities with large numbers of *economic* and racial minorities police would behave in an oppressive fashion. . . . It's not that *class conflict* alone can help us better understand police behavior but only that it . . . is one element that must be considered (Galliher 1971: 71; italics added).

In summarizing the literature, Brooks (1993: 150–155) states, "Police have a tendency to be and act suspicious of residents in lower-class neighborhoods. [Also] . . . It is generally supported in the literature that individuals in the lower socioeconomic strata receive harsher treatment by the police." Therefore the neighborhood, specifically its level of wealth, is one extralegal factor that is measured on the questionnaire to determine if it has an impact on police legal behavior.

The Police Culture

The concept of the police culture is the informal code of conduct that emphasizes "the danger and unpredictability of the work environment, the consequent dependence of officers on each other for assistance and protection, officers' autonomy in handling situations and the need to assert and maintain one's authority (Westley, 1970; Brown, 1981; Skolnick, 1966)" (Worden, 1992: 11).

Manning (1978: 9–13) offers a list of the distinctive aspects that make up this informal code and, therefore, the police culture:

(1) People cannot be trusted; they are dangerous. (2) Experience is better than abstract rules. (3) You must make people respect you. (4) Everyone hates a cop. (5) The legal system is untrustworthy; policemen make the best decisions about guilt or innocence. (6) People who are not controlled will break laws. (7) Policemen must appear respectable and be efficient. (8) Policemen can most accurately identify crime and criminals. (9) The major jobs of the policeman are to prevent crime and to enforce laws. (10) Stronger punishment will deter criminals from repeating their errors.

These distinctive aspects can be combined with similar insights in order to develop our understanding of how police legal behavior will be affected by the police culture. Several key aspects of the police culture are particularly important to our understanding of the law with respect to police. These aspects are used in the questionnaire to measure the impact of the culture compared to the law. One criterion is known as the "attitude test." Many authors have suggested that this test is one of the most important predictors of how police will handle a situation (e.g., Brown, 1981; Riksheim and Chermak, 1993; Black, 1970; Bayley, 1986; Lundman, 1974; Sykes and Clark, 1975; Westley, 1970). Very basically, the police culture demands that officers maintain respect. If a suspect does not show respect for an officer (failing the attitude test), the chances increase that the officer will take some sort of action, legal or not. For example, if a suspect calls an officer an "asshole," the attitude effect hypothesis would predict an increased chance that the officer will take some sort of action against that person in order to maintain respect.[4]

A second aspect of the police culture (or any culture) is its distinctive language. To measure this concept in the questionnaire, I asked a group of New York City officers to write words commonly used by police officers and familiar to them. Three such words were chosen to measure this aspect of the police culture in New York City: "skell," "mope," and "dirt-bag." These slang words are typical of police jargon in New York City. The connotations these words have to officers in the New York City Police Department are somewhat unique to that Department.[5] In general, the meaning of these words is basically a person who is considered to be repugnant, obnoxious, or acting in a nonconformist manner. Each of these words has a distinctive meaning. For example, according to the *Dictionary of Crime: Criminal Justice, Criminology and Law Enforcement* (1992), a mope is "a policeman's sarcastic term for a person with a long record of petty crimes such as shoplifting." The dictionary points out, that this is exclusively a New York City Police Department term. It is quite likely that officers would use extralegal measures against a person described in this way (Van Maanen, 1978).

The police culture is measured by a third aspect as well. Police officers are apt to react negatively to situations in which the suspect is a known "cop fighter." This is likely to evoke the strongest reactions from officers. There are at least two reasons for this. First, such a suspect does not show any respect to police and, therefore, fails the attitude test. Second, this suspect also evokes a sense of loyalty among officers because a fellow officer is involved. The literature has clearly developed this theme as being central to the police culture (e.g., Reuss-Ianni, 1983; Worden, 1992; Brown, 1981). The police culture, then, is measured by three key elements: (1) the attitude test (maintaining respect or demeanor), (2) the common and distinctive language of the New York City police culture, and (3) the idea of watching out for one another (loyalty).

The Police Bureaucracy

"The police bureaucracy" refers to formal department rules, guidelines, and procedures. Most important, it includes communications by street-level supervisors, who represent the agency at the local level, to officers in the field. How these supervisors interpret and communicate rules to officers may be of more consequence than the actual written policy (see especially Bayley and Bittner, 1984).[6] One supposedly powerful influence on officers' behavior is supervisory messages. Supervisors' instructions reflect the will of the police organization. Bayley and Bittner (1984: 109–113), for example, discuss the influence of ranking officers when they write, "Supervisors indicate—sometimes subtly, sometimes directly—what they prefer by way of action." Additionally, Brown (1981) feels that patrolmen are caught between the demands of an ambiguous task and a demand for conformity by administrators. We will measure the police organization in the questionnaire by using comments of a commanding officer at a fictitious roll call (before officers begin their tour of duty, they gather in a room and a supervisor gives assignments and information).

The commanding officer (C.O.) represents very high formal authority to precinct officers. The C.O. generally holds the rank of captain (sometimes higher ranks fill the position). To be promoted to the rank

of captain a police officer must pass three rigorous competitive civil service examinations that test his or her knowledge of formal rules and regulations. All advancement above the rank of captain is discretionary (i.e.,
he or she must be appointed by the Police Commissioner to that rank).[7]

The power of the C.O. is more direct than that of many other posi-
tions of formal authority. The C.O. ultimately decides all the operations
of the command, including, in many instances, who will receive choice
assignments. The C.O. is held responsible for all precinct operations, especially for increases/decreases in crime (e.g., Compstat), civilian complaints, arrests, summonses, and so on. Thus, messages from the C.O.
have powerful implications that should ultimately affect officers' behavior
(see also Mastrofski et al., 1995).

Up to this point, discussion has involved three key extralegal factors
that supposedly influence officer behavior: the community, the police
culture, and the police bureaucracy. However, the most important factor
to be measured is the law. Understanding basic legal concepts is, therefore, necessary before we can analyze the importance of these other factors and attempt to develop an understanding of various critical legal issues
in policing. Developing an understanding of the law and its measurement
are the topics of the next two sections.

Measurement of the Law: Police Stops

The legal power to forcibly stop criminal suspects is rooted in the
United States Supreme Court case *Terry v. Ohio* (1968). Based on this
case—and now codified in New York State in the Criminal Procedure Law
(see §140.50)—a police officer has the power to, if necessary, forcibly stop
and question a person regarding his/her conduct if the officer at least
reasonably suspects that the aforementioned person is committing, has
committed, or is about to commit a certain crime (specifically, for New
York City officers, felonies and misdemeanors defined in the New York
State Penal Law).[8] Essentially this means that officers, based on reasonable suspicion, may conduct a stop using force—which, generally, must
be short in duration and not very intrusive—to determine if a person is
engaging in illegal activity. In New York State, reasonable suspicion is
defined as "the quantum of knowledge sufficient to induce an ordinarily
prudent and cautious man under the circumstances to believe criminal
activity is at hand" (*People v. Cantor*, cited in NYPD, *Legal Bureau Bulletin* 5, no. 3 [1975]: 3).

Under certain limited circumstances, an officer may also conduct a frisk
(pat down of outer garments). In essence, the frisk may be done if the
officer reasonably suspects the suspect has a weapon. A search (going

inside the garments of the suspect—e.g., pockets, waistband, etc.) may also be done under limited circumstances. Basically, if the officer reasonably suspects an item found during the frisk could be a weapon, the officer may search the person. For example, if a police officer receives a call over the police radio indicating a white male in his twenties, wearing a green jacket, just robbed a store at gunpoint, then that police officer may stop, question, and frisk a person fitting that description who is in the area at that time.

The power to stop suspects is constantly being interpreted by the courts. Two court cases are used here to test New York City police officers' reactions to stop situations; one is based on a bright-line car stop case and another on an ambiguous person stop decision. For our purposes, a bright-line case is one that incorporates a clear, sensible rule which apparently offers effective guidance to law enforcement. An ambiguous case is one that apparently offers little guidance to law enforcement, contains at least one important term that is weakly defined, and has a rationale that tends to be weak or even senseless.[9] The dichotomy, of bright-line versus non-bright-line is suggested by numerous authors (e.g., Amsterdam, 1974; Butterfoss, 1988; Heffernan and Lovely, 1991; LaFave, 1993; Reinharz, 1996; Whitebread, 1985).

The bright-line court case is drawn from the United States Supreme Court case *Delaware v. Prouse* (1979). A hypothetical scenario to be included in the questionnaire was constructed from this case that involves stopping a vehicle without any suspicion of illegal activity. The stop is ostensibly being conducted to check an operator's license and vehicle registration. This is illegal per the *Prouse* decision. Specifically, officers are asked whether or not they would stop a car without any suspicion.

The ambiguous or non-bright-line scenario is constructed using a New York State Court of Appeals case, *People v. Martinez* (1992). In *Martinez* the New York State high court held that officers may *pursue* an individual for questioning only if there is reasonable suspicion that a person is about to commit a crime (more specifically, is committing, has committed, or is about to commit a crime).[10] The ambiguity in this case begins with a lack of a definition for "pursue," a word for which there are many connotations and denotations. For example, paraphrasing some of the definitions of "pursue" in *Webster's New Universal Unabridged Dictionary*: to chase; to follow close; to proceed in accordance with a plan; to continue to annoy; to continue a course of action; to follow; to continue; et cetera. Thus, the lack of clarity in the court's explanation may mean that officers may (or may not) keep the fleeing person under observation, follow the person, et cetera. We simply do not know.

The court's lack of an explanation of the word "pursue" was compounded by a failure to state what course of action officers *may* take, absent reasonable suspicion, if an individual runs from them. Furthermore, the court's reasoning is unclear, unconvincing, and debatable leaving officers even more confused. For example, the court wrote:

> Illustrative [of the many types of encounters by police] is police action which *restricts* an individual's freedom of movement by pursuing one who, for what ever reason, is fleeing to avoid police contact. *Because the resulting infringement on freedom of movement is similar, both forcible stops and pursuits require the same degree of information to justify them.* (*People v. Martinez;* italics added)

The court's reasoning here seems drastically flawed. First, it reasons that the mere act of pursuit (not defined) restricts a person's conduct. Is this true? Not necessarily. In many instances suspects are totally unaware that officers are in pursuit (e.g., plainclothes officers).

Second, it reasons that pursuit (whatever it means) will necessarily involve a "similar" level of infringement as a forcible stop. Is this true? Again, not necessarily. Officers can "pursue" with the intention of observing or following a suspect (as long as they do not forcibly stop and question). For example, officers may simply want to gather more information to develop a higher level of suspicion. The objective of the pursuit may not be, as the court seems to assume, to forcibly stop and question the suspect at this time, but rather to observe, follow, keep a watchful eye on a possible dangerous suspect/situation, or perhaps gain more information to raise the level of suspicion.

Third, and most egregious, we are given no guidance as to whether a pursuit is defined from the suspect's or officer's point of view or both. For example, let's say an officer decides to keep a suspect under observation with the intention of only following. Yet the person being observed, fearing the officer's following activity, gets scared and runs. In the process, that person throws narcotics to the ground. From the officer's point of view, it was not a pursuit. However, the suspect may have viewed it as such. Who, if anyone, is correct? What if the officer initially intended to forcibly stop the person? Would that mean it was a pursuit from the beginning? Questions such as these show that the court has left officers with little, if any, guidance.

Other court rulings in this area of law also show that the judiciary has had difficulty with it. In *Illinois v. Wardlow* (2000) both defense and prosecution argued strongly for bright-line rules in this area of the law. The United States Supreme Court, however, refused to adopt a bright-line rule but instead adopted a "totality of the circumstances" approach. Illinois argued that the Court should authorize temporary detention of anyone who runs upon seeing a police officer. Conversely, the defense argued for the opposite clear rule: that running upon seeing a police officer can never justify a stop (see especially Justice Stevens's dissent).

Before this case, the Supreme Court seemed poised to develop a bright-line in this area (see especially *California v. Hodari D.* [1991]) that would have favored Illinois. In *Hodari D.* the Court wrote in a 7–2 decision "that it would be unreasonable to stop, for brief inquiry, young men who scatter in panic upon the mere sighting of the police is not self evident, and arguably contradicts proverbial common sense, 'The wicked flee when no man pursueth.'"[11] Although the United States Supreme Court rejected the bright-line approach, at least it sensibly argued in *Wardlow* that "Headlong flight—wherever it occurs—is the consummate act of evasion: it is not necessarily indicative of wrongdoing, but it is certainly suggestive of such."

As we can see, even the judiciary is divided and unclear. For our purposes, the New York court in *Martinez* is ambiguous in guiding law enforcement by not allowing officers to "pursue" (whatever it means) those who flee them.[12] Given the lack of clear guidance for law enforcement in *Martinez* (i.e., no direction as to what officers can do, no explanation as to what a pursuit is, statements equating forcible stops with pursuits, no information as to whether the officer's or the suspect's point of view [or both] is controlling, and perhaps even defying common sense), the meaning of this case is ambiguous (perhaps purposely).

A hypothetical scenario on this case was created and administered to officers in the questionnaire. It involves a person running from an officer upon seeing the officer, who is easily identifiable because he is wearing a uniform. The question asks the respondents whether they would "*run after*" the suspect. Because the court said it is illegal to pursue, "*running after*" the person definitely is highly questionable behavior that, at a minimum, violates the spirit of the decision. However, running after the suspect may not be illegal. That is, if the officer merely *runs after* the person—say, to keep that person under observation—it may or may not be illegal.

Nevertheless, running after someone without reasonable suspicion is at least highly questionable for New York officers. This is a difficulty with ambiguous cases. That is, since the permissible behavior is left unclear by the courts, it is a vexing problem to determine the extent to which officers are violating that decision (see especially Johnson and Canon, 1984: 54). The meaning of *Martinez* is so questionable as to make it difficult to write a scenario that is absolutely illegal without using the specific words of the court (e.g., pursuit). The hypothetical question is *apparently illegal,* but without the court's guidance, *we just don't know for sure.*

Measurement of the Law: Search and Seizure

To determine how search and seizure law influences New York City officers, scenarios based on New York State court cases were utilized. For these cases, four hypothetical situations for each court case (on search and seizure) were constructed (rather than one situation created for each stop case). Each search and seizure situation corresponded to a level of the law: legal, illegal, slightly ambiguous, intensely ambiguous. The legal level is a hypothetical scenario in which the officer has the authority to do the act asked about. The illegal level is a scenario in which the officer does not have the authority to engage in the act asked about. The two middle level scenarios are purposely left unclear (the point of law itself was ambiguous in these areas) as to whether the officer has the authority to perform the act asked about. I will specifically explain these scenarios and give the legal background to them. The cases that were used are *People v. Jackson* (1992) and *People v. Gokey* (1983).

People v. Jackson

In *Jackson*, the New York State high court held that an officer may reach into a vehicle to determine if an object is a weapon, based on reasonable suspicion, only if the object is within the suspect's immediate grasp and the suspect is in the car. The rationale of the case indicated that the court made two critical distinctions. The first was the difference between a suspect being inside or outside the car. The court wrote:

> Contrary to defendant's contention, our holding in *People v. Torres* 74 N.Y.2d 224, 544 N.Y.S.2d 796, 543 N.E.2d 61, does not dictate a contrary result. There, the police proceeded to search a bag located on the front seat of a car that they had just stopped *after the suspect had been removed from the vehicle.* . . . Here, by contrast, the rather cursory examination of the bag occurred *while the defendant was still sitting in the car.*

The second distinction was between the possible weapon being within the suspect's grasp or not within the suspect's grasp. The court wrote, "Since . . . the bag was still within defendant's reach, the police were justified in examining it."

Thus, this case means that an officer may search a vehicle, based on reasonable suspicion, only if the suspect is in the automobile and the

Table 2.1
Summary of Measurement of the Law

POLICE STOPS

Court cases	Scenarios	Legality of Scenarios
Delaware v. *Prouse*	One (1) bright-line car stop	(1) illegal
People v. *Martinez*	One (1) ambiguous person stop	(1) probably illegal

SEARCH AND SEIZURE

Court cases	Scenarios	Legality of Scenarios
People v. *Jackson*	Four (4) search for weapon situations	(1) legal (1) modestly ambiguous (1) highly ambiguous (1) illegal
People v. *Gokey*	Four (4) search for drug situations	(1) legal (1) modestly ambiguous (1) highly ambiguous (1) illegal

Note: See Appendix for exact wording of each situation.

possible weapon is within the suspect's immediate grasp. Interestingly, a more recent case, *People v. Carvey* (1997), indicates that the court will decide, on a case-by-case analysis, exceptions to this. In *Carvey* the court, based on facts very specific to the case, held that a search of the car, based on reasonable suspicion, when the suspects are outside the vehicle may be upheld if the weapon poses an actual and specific danger to officer safety.[13] This was a marked departure from the state court's previous opinion and was decided after the questionnaire was distributed. The *Carvey* case clearly illustrates the court's capriciousness on this issue.

Four specific hypothetical situations at different levels of legality (from legal to illegal) were constructed utilizing the two main aspects of the *Jackson* case. The completely legal scenario was constructed so that the hypothetical situation clearly develops to the level of reasonable suspicion. The scenario starts off with a person who "fits the description of a robbery suspect." Furthermore, the suspect is still inside the car and is on a street known for criminal activity. The apparent gun is "right next to the suspect," obviously within reach. These criteria clearly meet the court's requirements in *Jackson* (i.e., reasonable suspicion, suspect in car, gun within reach), making the level completely legal for officers to search the vehicle.

The slightly ambiguous scenario purposely outlines a situation in which it is somewhat unclear as to whether officers might legally be able to enter the auto in order to conduct a search. At this level the person does not fit the description of a robbery suspect, is neither fully in nor fully out of the car, and the gun is now "next to the driver's seat." More specifically, as the officer approaches the auto, the driver begins to get out of the vehicle and is standing with one foot on the pavement and the other in the car. The court does not address the issue of whether officers may legally search a car when a person is neither fully in nor fully out of the vehicle. Also, the apparent gun is next to the driver's seat. It is not entirely clear whether the person could immediately grasp it. Given these circumstances, officers are asked whether they would search or not.

For the highly ambiguous scenario, the situation becomes even more convoluted as to whether it is legally permissible to conduct a search of the auto. As with the slightly ambiguous situation, the person does not fit the description of a robbery suspect and is not fully in or fully out of the car (one foot on pavement and the other in the car). However, the weapon is now even further away (i.e., in the rear seat on the passenger side), making it more difficult for the person to get to it.

In the clearly illegal scenario, the suspect is within walking distance of the car but plainly far enough away not to be able to grab for the weapon. Since the person is not a suspect, is completely out of the vehicle, and is not even remotely able to grab the gun, it is clearly not permissible for officers to conduct a search of the vehicle. Furthermore, the person has made no furtive movements and is "casually walking to an apartment to ring a doorbell." This vividly demonstrates that the person represents no apparent immediate danger, and therefore officers cannot search the car for a weapon.

People v. Gokey

The second case that was used to develop search and seizure legal scenarios was *People v. Gokey*. The court in *Gokey* held that a container on a person that is within the immediate control or grabbable area of a suspect at the time of arrest cannot be subjected to a warrantless search incident to arrest, unless the circumstances leading to the arrest support a reasonable belief that the suspect may gain possession of a weapon or be able to destroy evidence located in the bag. (Confused? So is everyone else.) The New York Court of Appeals in this case rejected the bright-line rule of the Supreme Court of the United States that an arrest justifies the search of containers within the immediate control or reach of a person (see especially *Chimel v. California* [1969]).

The New York State Court of Appeals constructed an exception to the *Gokey* case in *People v. Smith* (1983). In *Smith* the New York State Court basically held that mere arrest does not justify the search of a container; however, when the facts of a particular case indicate that there is reason to suspect that the arrested person may be armed and the search is close in time to the arrest, a search of a container may be permissible (to be determined case by case). The major point of the *Gokey/Smith* cases is that containers which are portable cannot be searched unless there is a reasonable belief that the evidence may be destroyed or a weapon may be obtained (NYCPD, 1997c: Chapter 12, 12). In this case, the New York court created a new level of proof somewhere below reasonable suspicion but above mere suspicion (no evidence, just an intuition or hunch), adding another layer of confusion to an already convoluted area of law.

Different hypothetical situations corresponding to the level of legality were also constructed using the *Gokey/Smith* cases. The legal scenario contained information which clearly indicated to officers that it was legally permissible to conduct a search. The suspect is a known drug dealer; he is immediately arrested and has the unlocked duffel bag in his hand; a nearby fire in a garbage can (which is typical on cold days) is clearly a threat to the evidence; and the search is to be done immediately and in the arrestee's presence, as suggested by the NYPD's Legal Bureau.

The slightly ambiguous scenario contained information that leaves the situation somewhat unclear as to whether officers may search the duffel bag. The suspect is a known drug dealer, the duffel bag is on the ground between the suspect's legs and is not being carried by the suspect, and the officer immediately seizes the bag. The legal question for officers is whether or not there is a threat to officer safety or to evidence. Since the scenario involves a known drug dealer, most of whom are dangerous, the officer might be able to articulate the need to search the bag. On the other hand, there is no immediate threat to officer safety or to the evidence, and therefore the officer could get a search warrant and merely seize the bag (similar to the *Gokey* case). Thus, the situation is slightly ambiguous.

In the extremely ambiguous situation the suspect is not a known drug dealer, the bag is now locked shut (although a key is immediately available), the duffel bag is on the ground between the suspect's legs and is not being carried, other officers are present (lessening the threat somewhat), and the officer has already frisked the person without seizing the bag (indicating a lack of a threat from the bag). All these facts taken together leave the situation very unclear as to whether officers could legally search the duffel bag.

In the illegal scenario officers clearly do not have the lawful authority to search the bag. In this situation, the suspect is not a known drug dealer, the briefcase is locked shut without a key available, the case is on the ground between the suspect's legs and is not being carried, several other officers are present, and the crime committed is very minor (i.e., possession of a small amount of marijuana). Under these circumstances, officers do not have the power to search the briefcase but may arrest the individual, seize the briefcase, and then get a search warrant.[14]

Factorial Survey: A Complete Vignette

These explanations about court cases are very important because they allow us to measure the extent to which the judiciary checks police power. Complete hypothetical street situations (vignettes) were created using these legal situations and combining them with other factors (community, police culture, and police bureaucracy). Questions on the survey, then, combine all four factors. An example of a typical question is the following:

At roll call the Captain states, "Civilian complaints have increased." You then go on patrol in a wealthy neighborhood. During the tour you observe a cooperative individual who you know to be a drug dealer. He places what appears to be 100 marijuana cigarettes into an unlocked duffel bag. You immediately arrest the suspect who is holding the zippered shut duffel bag in his hand on a crowded streetcorner. You realize that the bag could easily be destroyed by throwing it into a nearby fire in a garbage can. Immediately, fearing destruction of the evidence, you take the bag from his hand. Would you without delay, at the arrest site, and in the presence of the arrestee, look inside the unlocked duffel bag?

The Captain's statement about civilian complaints is from the police bureaucracy. The wealthy neighborhood is measuring the impact of the community. The cooperative individual (as opposed to a "mope" or "asshole") is measuring the police culture. Last, the part about the fire and the duffel bag are based on the law (court case; this one is from *People v. Gokey*).

In this way, various questions were created and distributed to officers. They answered these vignettes on a scale of 1 to 8, with 1 being definitely not doing the behavior and 8 being definitely doing the behavior. As we shall see, the impact of each factor on officers' stop and search behavior can now be determined. Since these mimic street situations, we are tapping into officers' decision-making processes.[15]

Other Important Aspects of the Questionnaire

There are two other parts to the questionnaire that utilize more traditional measures. One part includes measures of officers' attitudes, such as selectiveness and aggressiveness. There are seven of this type of question. The last part of the questionnaire contains six questions aimed at collecting background information on the respondent (e.g., age, sex, education level). Once completed, the survey was distributed to a randomly selected sample of New York City police officers working in precincts. There were 1,259 usable surveys returned out of 2,052 sent. This represents a 61 percent return rate—very good for a survey of government workers in a large city.[16] (For a more detailed description of the questions and the questionnaire, see the Appendix.)

Representativeness

An important aspect of a survey is that the sample should be representative of the population being studied. Based on the self-reported characteristics of those returning the surveys, the sample certainly seems representative of New York City precinct officers. The average age of precinct officers who work in precincts is 32.3 years.[17] The average age of the sample is 31.7 years. The average tenure of New York City precinct officers is 7.1 years. The average tenure of the sample is 7.6 years. The percentages of male and female police officers who work in precincts are 83.6 percent and 16.4 percent, respectively. In the sample the percentages of male and female officers are 81.4 percent and 18.6 percent. Of particular concern is achieving a representative sample of those officers who have no more than a high school education. The percentage of precinct officers with a high school education is 37.2 percent. The percentage of officers with a high school education in the sample is 31.7 percent.[18] These percentages certainly suggest that the sample is highly representative of precinct officers.

NEW YORK CITY AND ITS LEGAL TRAINING FOR POLICE

Making reasonable assessments about the police officers' responses to the questions requires an understanding of New York City and its police training. For example, one could ask whether police in New York City have any knowledge whatsoever of these court cases. If they do not, then it would be reasonable to assume that it is lack of knowledge, and not officer discretion, contributing to police misconduct. This section provides basic information about New York City and its police, with particular emphasis on how police officers are trained to handle these legal situations.

New York City has five boroughs (counties), covering 322 square miles, and many communities. According to the 2000 census, the city has a population of approximately 8 million, with an ethnic breakdown of 25 percent black, 27 percent Hispanic, 35 percent white, and 13 percent Asian/other. There are over 30 million visitors each year. Just about every type of situation, individual, or place is represented.

The NYPD divides the five boroughs into eight patrol boroughs: Manhattan South, Manhattan North, the Bronx, Brooklyn South, Brooklyn North, Queens South, Queens North, and Staten Island. Working within the framework of the NYPD, these commands have created some of their own rules to address specific problems within their particular patrol borough. Additionally, there are 76 patrol precincts within the 8 borough commands, 9 housing police service areas (how the police geographically divide the public housing facilities), and 12 transit districts (how the police geographically divide the transit system, subways). The NYPD consists of approximately 40,000 uniformed officers. Of these, about 26,500 are police officers.

Before prospective officers are hired and sent to the Police Academy for training, they are carefully screened. This begins with a civil service test, which is a multiple choice (pen and paper) test that helps determine candidates' abilities to perform the job of police officer. Candidates must also pass medical, physical, psychological, and background screenings. Recent changes in hiring standards now require New York City officers to have completed two years of college or have two years of military experience before being appointed.

If all the candidate screenings are passed, recruits enter the Police Academy. Training for New York City officers is intense.[19] In fact, Police Academy training in New York City is generally considered the equivalent of approximately 30 undergraduate college credits. Recruits are trained for approximately six months (not including field training) in police science, behavioral science, law, physical education, and firearms. In the law curriculum, at a minimum, there is an attempt to communicate legal constraints to officers. As Bayley (1994: 66) states, "Police have no choice but to pay close attention to constitutions, statutes, and judicial opinions. . . . Indeed, in recent years the demands for accountability to law and public opinion have intensified in democratic countries." As an example, New York City police officer recruits are given approximately 172 hours (this includes workshops, role playing, etc.) of training in the law (NYCPD, 1997b). The legal study material for student officers is 57 chapters long (NYCPD, 1997b). It contains detailed information ranging from constitutional principles to specific offenses.

Prospective officers must attain at least a 70 percent grade in law and an overall grade of 75 percent to graduate the Academy. Additionally, the New York City Police Department has numerous other training sessions (borough-based training, precinct level training, etc.), and officers receive updated *Legal Bureau Bulletins* that summarize new laws and cases for them. Furthermore, all New York City officers must take an oath to uphold the United States Constitution. Of course, all this means is that officers *should* be guided by the legal restrictions on their power. In the following chapters, specific issues with respect to the impact of the law on police are outlined. The questionnaire and this background information will be the basis for much of the information in the following chapters.

SUMMARY

Studying the impact of the procedure law on police power is complicated by the fact that most stops and searches take place under very cloaked circumstances (often, neither a supervisor nor a witness is present). To study police officers' legal behavior, social science techniques including a scientifically designed questionnaire (that contains hypothetical situations), combined with 20 years of practical experience with the NYPD, are utilized. Three extralegal factors are examined in the first part of the questionnaire: the community, the police culture, and the police bureaucracy. Specific aspects of each are studied. For example, community wealth, the attitude effect, and the influence of supervisors are underlying elements of the community, the culture, and the bureaucracy, respectively. To measure the impact of the law, situations based on police stops and on search and seizure court cases are used. A hypothetical question, called a vignette, is then formed by combining aspects of the three extralegal influences (community, police culture, and police bureaucracy) with a legal situation (from court cases). Assessment of officers' judgments on these questions allows researchers to determine the extent of the influence of the law on officers' decisions (e.g., to search or not). The final two parts of the questionnaire allow for testing of the impact of officers' attitudes and characteristics. Background information about New York City and the NYPD's recruitment and training demonstrate that, at a minimum, officers are well versed in legal standards.

NOTES

1. It is important to understand and appreciate that these explanations are extremely condensed. The specifics, for example, of the areas of the law such as stop and frisk and search and seizure are questioned by even the most learned judicial authorities. Consequently, this work will not explain every intricacy of these concepts; this is well beyond its scope.

2. Observations may be less appropriate to the current study because observers of police—perhaps merely by their presence, no matter how seemingly innocuous—may influence the legal behavior of the officers/suspects they are watching (e.g., cause officers to search more or less often; influence a suspect to be more hostile or contrite); the minimally trained observer's eye may not capture vital information necessary to expose the root cause of a legal behavior (e.g., a furtive movement by a suspect in a crowd; a bulge in a pocket); and the cost to conduct a proper observational study is relatively high in both time and money.

3. Validity and reliability of this original instrument were measured during a pretest and found to be well within acceptable parameters.

4. However, see Klinger (1994) for an opposing argument.

5. To use this instrument with other police departments would require adjustments in wording, since other departments have their own distinctive language (as well as different laws, bureaucracies, etc.).

6. The written policies of most concern to this study are those which involve legal decisions. Because these policies are basically written by the courts and repeated by police departments, they are included under the legal variable.

7. The Police Commissioner is the person in overall command of the New York City Police Department. This person is appointed at the discretion of the mayor. The Commissioner is a civilian who may not necessarily have served as a police officer. If a person does rise through the ranks to become Commissioner,

that person must resign from the Police Department or take a leave of absence from uniformed service.

8. There are other criteria and case law that make this much more complicated. For example, an officer must be in his/her geographical area of employment (for New York City officers, it is the New York City area). See New York State CPL §140.50 (1).

9. A case can be bright-line on one issue but ambiguous on certain points.

10. Note that this decision was favorable for the police, in that the defense was arguing that officers need probable cause to pursue.

11. In this type of situation, where New York courts give more rights than the U.S. Supreme Court, based on the New York State Constitution, the New York court's decision becomes law *only in New York State*.

12. This is a more far-reaching (and less clear) decision compared to the United States Supreme Court's, which does not permit a "forcible stop" under similar circumstances.

13. In that case, the suspect was wearing a bullet-resistant vest.

14. Note that one scenario used weapons and the other, drugs. This was by design. Since we are studying legal police behavior, we want to capture (where possible) illegal behavior by officers. Therefore, based on previous research suggesting that officers are *most* likely to conduct an illegal search in weapon and drug situations (see especially Heffernan and Lovely, 1991; Nardulli, 1983), these situations were utilized. Also, if necessary, we can look at the stop scenarios and compare the results with the search and seizure situations if deemed appropriate. One final point: as stated earlier, using weapon/drug scenarios means that the illegal activity measured should be considered, if anything, a high estimate of officers' illegal activity.

15. The measures utilized for this study certainly pass the threshold of face validity. Although face validity is generally acceptable for a study of this type, the current research went the extra step. For this study, criterion-related validity was developed utilizing a pretest. A pretest was distributed on January 25, 1994, to a stratified (by precinct and borough) random sample of 50 officers from five precincts. The validity is accomplished by showing a correlation between the judgments about the hypothetical scenarios and a known criterion of officers' actual field behavior at the same point in time (also called *concurrent validity*). This is precisely what is found. A measure of officers' evaluations called apprehension/intervention has a statistically significant and modest correlation with the officers' judgments ($r = -.19$, $p < .002$). The negative correlation is exactly what is expected; as officers' judgments become illegal (higher scores are illegal judgments on the pretest), their evaluations go down (an inverse relationship). This relationship between the evaluations and the judgments is important statistical evidence showing that the scenarios are measuring how officers respond in the field. Although this is only a modest correlation, it is neither unusual nor unexpected in survey research (see Bohrnstedt, 1983: 97–98).

16. Note, however, that this study does not utilize a *simple* random sampling design but uses a *stratified* random sampling design with replacement, stratified

by precinct. That is, I selected twenty-seven officers and twenty-seven alternates randomly from each of the seventy-six precincts. The alternates were selected in case of transfer, vacation, sickness, or refusal to complete the instrument. This is one way in which the return rate was increased.

17. All statistics regarding the New York City Police Department are as of March 1, 1998, and were supplied by the NYCPD's Office of Management Analysis and Planning.

18. Both the Police Department figure and the sample figure for high school graduates includes officers with an equivalency diploma (G.E.D.).

19. Training continues to expand in this area as the department continually monitors the legal situation for new needs (e.g., the stop and frisk procedure was updated on January 1, 2001).

CHAPTER 3

The Influence of Courts on Police Power

Not much is known about the extent to which court rulings are obeyed. What is known of judicial impact, particularly as it relates to policing, is limited and much of it is anecdotal. For example, in a comprehensive study of the United States Supreme Court, Segal and Spaeth (1993: xv) state, "Sad to say, political scientists tend to discard science when the Court is their subject."

Those who have studied judicial impact are exceedingly diversified in their views especially with regard to police. Historians have suggested that the courts, especially since the 1960s and 1970s, have had an enormous influence on police (e.g., Kelly et al., 1983: 643–645; Nevins and Commager, 1986: 553). Some legal scholars also maintain that the courts are influencing the police. For example, Johnson and Canon (1984: 251) state, "It might be argued that the courts, and especially the Supreme Court, have had greater success in altering behavior in the criminal justice area than in any other."

Others assert that the police are, at best, only marginally influenced by the courts. Manning (1977: 101), for example, argues that "the law serves as a mystification device or canopy to cover selectively, legitimate, and rationalize police conduct. It does not prospectively guide police action, nor does it provide the principal constraint upon police practices." Westley (1970: 141) feels that "They [police] recognize that it [the law] sets limits to their actions. . . . Yet, when contrasted to other ends, it plays a subordinate role." Skolnick and Fyfe (1993: xvi, 193–194) point out:

In the popular view, perhaps the most frequent check on day-to-day police operations is the criminal courts, which in theory see to it that police anticrime efforts conform to the Constitution. The right to be free from unreasonable search, the right to remain silent, the right to an attorney. . . . Neither practice and theory nor reality and perception always match, however, and the general conception of the courts' influence on police activity is exaggerated. The exclusionary rule, for example, is no bar to the search practices of officers.

LIMITED VERSUS UNLIMITED GOVERNMENT

Determining the extent of the judiciary's influence—or lack of influence—on police behavior has important implications for our government. One important way to assess the extent to which the democratic process of government is functioning is to examine police behavior with respect to procedure law. To that end, the police have been seen by many as the focal point of democracy at work. For example, Bouza (1990: 171–172) writes, "There is no doubt that making the state more efficient usually means making it more powerful. . . . The push-pull of individual freedoms and the power of the state form the central dilemma of political life in society. It's never more dramatically illustrated [than] surrounding the operation of police departments." And Manning (1978: 29) states, "The problem of the police is, essentially, the problem of democratic society."

Law enforcement officers in democratic countries are theoretically constrained by the law and sworn to uphold the rights of all. That is, they must work within legal guidelines. In the United States, the executive branch, including the police, is supposedly kept in check by the judicial and legislative branches of government. The judiciary interprets the law, while the legislature creates the law. Former Chief Justice Earl Warren (1959: 89), for example, points out that, "Life and liberty can be as much endangered from illegal methods used to convict those thought to be criminals as from the actual criminals themselves." Hence, if the government is, in theory, functioning properly, the police must be following legal guidelines that restrict their power. This is the essence of our system of government.

As our discussion on procedure law advised, the Bill of Rights (the first ten amendments to the Constitution) is, theoretically, a guardian against abuses of police power (and other government authority). For example, former Justice William O. Douglas (1954: 71) stated, "The 5th Amendment is an old friend and a good friend . . . . one of the great landmarks in men's struggle to be free of tyranny, to be decent and civilized." The United States Supreme Court has made many parts of the Bill of Rights applicable to state and local police officers. They must uphold and abide by the restrictions indicated by the high Court.[1]

The courts have promulgated, and are promulgating, many guidelines with the express purpose of influencing police officers (e.g., search and seizure, stop and frisk). In particular, the remedy created by the courts to enforce many of these guidelines is exclusion. There are also many other ways in which our society tries to control police behavior: arrest of officers, civil suits, civilian complaints, discipline within a police agency. Because of these many sanctions, some experts argue that police are limited in power and that the aforementioned methods do indeed control police behavior.

In stark contrast to the view that police are controlled or limited in power, is the idea that the police can be so overwhelmingly powerful that they are the defining aspect of the entire government. This is known as a police state. A *police state* is defined (*Academic American Encyclopedia*, 1996) as

> a form of totalitarianism that is characterized by its reliance on a police force, usually secret, in order to suppress dissent. The Gestapo operating in Germany under Adolf Hitler, ostensibly to preserve the integrity of the state, was such a force, as were the KGB of the former USSR and Savak in Iran under the shah. Another example of a secret police organization is the Gong'an Bu (Kung-an Pu) in China. Secret police are given broad and loosely defined powers to root out political malcontents. Their victims are often secretly arrested, tried, and punished *without being afforded the usual protections of due process, even when those protections are ostensibly part of the country's legal procedure.* (Italics added)

Another example of a police state is presented by Burleigh and Wipperman (1991: 63). They describe the state of affairs for police as the Nazis came to power thus: "not only the Gestapo could detain people in 'protective custody,' but also the regular and criminal police, who could now keep the 'asocial' in 'police preventive custody.' This practice was retrospectively legalised on 14 December 1937 when Himmler issued a 'decree for the preventive fight against crime.'"

The idea that police in the United States are operating under their own set of laws (including, at times, comparing them to a police state) should not be underestimated. Many respected authors claim that the police in the United States are, at least to some extent, uncontrolled by legal guidelines (see especially Bittner, 1970; Chambliss, 1994; Manning, 1977; Skolnick, 1966; Skolnick and Fyfe, 1993; Westley, 1970). For example, Skolnick (1966: 144) writes, "The policeman does not feel legally constrained in conducting an exploratory examination of suspicious premises. Even less does he feel morally at fault in conducting a prior search. . . . The process by which the policeman justifies his unlawful exploratory search is similar to that by which many criminals justify theirs. The policeman distinguishes between legality and morality just as the criminal does." Skolnick clearly argues that police are uninfluenced by legal guidelines. Chambliss (1994: 192–193) is even more direct, claiming that due to police abuse of authority, the "United States will move towards a society divided by race and class into communities that are *quasi police states*" (italics added).

In New York City events such as the brutalizing of a Haitian immigrant, Abner Louima, are harsh reminders of what unlimited police power can mean. Mr. Louima was sexually abused by officers in a bathroom of a Brooklyn precinct. Specifically, an officer placed an object in the rectum of Mr. Louima, who was in custody at the time of the incident. Although the officer involved was arrested and convicted, such reprehensible acts could be interpreted to suggest that police, in general, do not follow the law. A logical question arises: are these isolated events, or are police by and large abusing their power? Commentary is widely available on both sides of the spectrum. For example, former Mayor Rudolph Giuliani stated, "If you really are a police officer of the City of New York, if you really understand what it means to be a police officer, if you really understand what it means to protect the lives of other people, then you will be among the most revulsed and repulsed by what happened here. If you don't understand that, then you really should leave the Police Department" (Barry, 1997: A1). Contrast that with statements by ordinary citizens who have been quoted as stating that people in New York City "are locked up because of their race or their politics, as in Nazi Germany" (Haberman, 1997: B1).

The horrific terrorist attack of September 11, 2001, also puts forth serious concerns about the extent of government power especially with respect to civil liberties. For example, according to Drew and Miller (2002), writing for the *New York Times*, "more than 700 people were held on immigration charges after Sept. 11." As of February 18, 2002, the government still held over three hundred of them in custody and eighty-seven of them already had court orders to leave the country. Little or no evidence of wrongdoing has been found against many of these people. How long should these people be held as detainees (not convicted of any crime) without a decision being made about deporting them, releasing them, or going to trial? There is a real concern when government power holds people with little or no evidence. Could we become a nation ruled by our fear of terrorism? The specter of a police officer asking for "your papers" does not seem farfetched. Our society needs to make reasonable decisions based on facts, not fear.

DEBATE ABOUT THE EXCLUSIONARY
RULE'S IMPACT

While research is generally sparse in the area of judicial impact, there is one exception—exclusionary rule research. The exclusionary rule is one area of judicial impact theory that has been profusely debated and studied. The plethora of literature on the exclusionary rule has inundated the field with information and data as well as comments and suggestions. Unfortunately, these studies, even the empirical ones, tend to contradict one another (often depending on the point of view of the author). For example, the outspoken defender of the exclusionary rule, Yale Kamisar (1990: 562), effectively sums up the point of view of the defenders: "I believe that originally and for much of its life the federal exclusionary rule rested not on an empirical proposition, but on what might be called a 'principled basis' (to avoid 'ratifying' the unconstitutional police conduct that produced the proffered evidence, to keep the judicial process from being contaminated by partnership in police misconduct, and to assure the police and the public alike that the Court took the fourth amendment seriously)."

Others feel that the exclusionary rule is not a good method for enforcing the Fourth Amendment. For example, Malcolm Richard Wilkey (1982: 17) states:

> The time has come to abolish the exclusionary rule . . . the exclusionary rule perversely insures that the wrongdoer, the police officer who conducted the illegal search, escapes punishment. . . . The search and seizure opinions of the Supreme Court for the last twenty years exhibit a reiteration by one Justice after another that this is a method of enforcing a constitutional protection, not necessarily the precise method commanded by the Constitution, but instead one chosen by the High Court.

Klotter and Kanovitz (1983: 177) quote Justice Benjamin Cardozo of the New York Court of Appeals, who is often cited by those against exclusion. Justice Cardozo commented, "The criminal is to go free because the constable has blundered" (*People v. Defore* [1926]). Both Wilkey and Cardozo are arguing that the exclusionary rule should be eliminated but from different viewpoints. Wilkey argues that the police officer is not punished, whereas Cardozo feels that the criminal is not.

Initial Studies

Initial studies on the exclusionary rule vehemently debate the need for the rule itself. Interestingly, evidence was gathered to indicate both points of view. Some of the earlier empirical studies on the exclusionary rule include Oaks (1970), Spiotto (1973), Schrock and Welsh (1974), Kaplan (1974), Hirschel (1977), Davies (1974), and Columbia Law School (1968). Four of these take the position that the exclusionary rule should be altered or abolished (Oaks, 1970; Spiotto, 1973; Kaplan, 1974; and Hirschel, 1977), while the remaining three (Columbia Law School, 1968; Davies, 1974; and Schrock and Welsh, 1974) assert that the exclusionary rule should basically remain intact. To develop a comprehensive understanding of the impact of the judiciary, as well as of the controversy surrounding the exclusionary rule debate, I will briefly review the main points of these studies.

Oaks's (1970) study is a comprehensive analysis of the impact of the exclusionary rule, including a summary of extant research. Oaks (1970: 709) reviewed the available literature on the topic, and stated that, "The foregoing findings represent the largest fund of information yet assembled on the effect of the exclusionary rule, but they obviously fall short of an empirical substantiation or refutation of the deterrent effect of the exclusionary rule." He subsequently attempted to study the issue himself, and pointed out, "In view of the complexity of the inquiry, it presently appears to be impossible to design any . . . tests that would give a reliable measure of the overall deterrent effect" (Oaks, 1970: 716).

Spiotto (1973) examined motions to suppress in Chicago. He found that there was a general increase in motions to suppress since the mid-1950s; that substantial court time in certain crimes, such as narcotics, was wasted on suppression hearings; and that narcotics and gun offenses were most likely to involve motions to suppress. He concluded by stating, "The sample is small but it seems to indicate that some police, at least, are not deterred by the exclusionary rule at all" (Spiotto, 1973: 277).

In a scathing criticism of Spiotto's study, Davies (1974) discussed some of the methodological flaws in Spiotto's research. One powerful criticism is that Spiotto partially used a before-after *Mapp v. Ohio* (1961) design to study how the introduction of the *exclusionary rule in Chicago* changed officer behavior. Spiotto apparently failed to account for the fact that *Illinois adopted the exclusionary rule in 1923, forty-eight years* before *Mapp*. In other words, Spiotto treated the "law" as a *constant.*[2]

One lesson to be learned from this is that the law varies greatly—from the national level to the state level, from jurisdiction to jurisdiction, and over time: it is *anything but* constant. Depending on the research question, a failure to account for this variation could ruin a well-intentioned study. Researchers must be particularly careful to look for these differing interpretations of the law (including interpretations of exactly the same language by different courts or interpretations by the same court at different times). For example, say we wish to study the impact of the so-called *plain touch* exception to the exclusionary rule. The plain touch exception basically means that when an officer is legally feeling the outer garments of a suspect (i.e., patting down), if that officer immediately recognizes, from the feel, that materials inside the clothing are illegal (such as crack vials), the materials may be seized and the person arrested. The United States Supreme Court created this exception in *Minnesota v. Dickerson* (1993). In conducting a study of the plain touch exception, researchers need to be aware (and design a study accordingly) that New York State does *not* recognize this exception (see *People v. Diaz* [1993]). This is so even though the "Fourth Amendment and the parallel New York State provision read *exactly the same*" (Reinharz, 1996: 42).[3]

In another study, Schrock and Welsh (1974) argue that an individual's opinion for or against exclusion will depend on that person's *view* of government. Those who argue in favor of the *unitary* model of government (i.e., all branches of government are united) will favor the exclusionary rule. Those who argue that the *fragmentary* model of government is correct (sometimes called the invasion theory of the amendment; each branch of government is separate and distinct) will not agree with the exclusionary rule. This is especially true because "The executive is the only branch of government to which the amendment speaks." (Schrock and Welsh, 1974: 289). Therefore, depending on one's point of view, an individual can either accept or reject exclusion.

More Recent Work

Some of the more recent empirical studies on the exclusionary rule include Nardulli (1983), Orfield (1987), Canon (1979), Loewenthal (1980), Sutton (1986), Uchida and Bynum (1991), and Heffernan and Lovely (1991). Nardulli (1983) studied felony prosecutions by examining criminal court data in nine medium-sized counties. He also interviewed many persons involved in the criminal justice system, with the notable exception of police officers. He concluded:

> Given the results of the empirical analysis it seems clear that the exclusionary rules . . . have a truly marginal effect on the criminal court system. . . . The costs of keeping the rules are not "the release of countless guilty criminals"; only a relatively few marginal offenders are released. If these minuscule costs are compared with the benefits (the ambiguous deterrence of the rules), I can only conclude that there should be no change in the status quo. (Nardulli, 1983: 606–607)

Additionally, similar to previous research in this area, he found that the highest success rates in motions to suppress are in drug and weapon charges.

Orfield (1987) suggests that the exclusionary rule deters officers. His study basically involved giving a questionnaire (in a structured interview) to a very small number (sample size [n] = 26) of Chicago narcotics officers. The survey was not anonymous, and asked numerous sensitive questions, such as "How often do you lie?" For these reasons, the validity of the results is certainly debatable (Babbie, 1989; Bradburn, 1983). The small sample also makes the results extremely suspect. Nevertheless, Orfield suggests that the results of the survey indicate that officers are deterred.

In another study, Canon (1979) utilized questionnaires sent to police departments that serve cities with populations over one hundred thousand. He received responses from over half of them. In the questionnaire, he asked departments to compare their present behavior with that in 1967. The departments reported the following information: agencies were using search warrants more often; departments had more restrictive policies regarding search and seizure; and, at the time of the survey, charges were "rarely" dropped (in court) due to illegal seizure of evidence. Canon suggested that the questionnaires show how the exclusionary rule was having a more effective impact at the time of his study compared to previous years. Additionally, he refuted the assertion that the evidence clearly shows police are not deterred. Canon (1979: 400) wrote:

> When the totality of the evidence is examined . . . it does not support the . . . conclusion that the rule is inefficacious in curbing illegal police searches. Neither . . . does the evidence support the opposite conclusion— that the rule deters police illegalities nearly 100 percent of the time. Put shortly, the rule has differential impact depending upon time and place.

Loewenthal (1980), in a study of New York City officers, suggests that police are deterred when the law is clear but that the pressures from ranking officers to make arrests and possibly violate the law are very strong. Loewenthal (1980: 32–35) states:

> Spurred by pressures for arrests from their commanders, police investigators are often tempted to violate the warrant and probable cause requirements of the fourth amendment in order to obtain enough evidence to substantiate a sufficient number of arrests. However, many police officers are apparently deterred from searches that are clearly illegal because of the problem created by the exclusionary rule.

In studying search warrant applications, Uchida and Bynum (1991: 1065) suggest that the exclusionary rule has a strong influence on police.[4]

> Our interviews indicated that police were willing to follow guidelines established by the Constitution, the district attorney's office, and the courts when writing search warrant applications. The willingness of officers in [some jurisdictions] . . . to have warrants reviewed by prosecutors was a response, in part, to the exclusionary sanction.

Heffernan and Lovely (1991) attempted to use more modern research methods to study the impact of the exclusionary rule. They utilized questionnaires administered to four mid-sized police departments in New England and one of the middle Atlantic states. Interestingly, they found that "53% of officers . . . showed unequivocal respect for the law by never indicating that they would intrude in a setting where they believed it illegal to do so" (Heffernan and Lovely, 1991: 351). Further, about 15 percent knowingly violated legal restrictions (Heffernan and Lovely, 1991: 348). However, the authors suggested that "complexity of the law imposes a substantial limitation on the possibility of deterring police illegality" (Heffernan and Lovely, 1991: 339).

Major points that can be extracted from these studies are the following: (1) information on the influence of state courts is woefully lacking; (2) theories on judicial impact are largely untested and developing; (3) conflicting information exists as to how *police* (i.e., frontline legal practitioners) react to court decisions; (4) methodological issues in this area need to be more closely addressed; (5) the law can be complex in this area; (6) there are some indications that training and education are important; (7) the evidence most likely to be suppressed involve weapons and drugs; (8) there is some anecdotal information as to what might influence officers to violate the law (e.g., pressure from supervisors); and (9) further research is needed.

In sum, several empirical studies claim that law enforcement officers are not deterred by the exclusionary rule (e.g., Oaks, 1970; Spiotto, 1973; Hirschel, 1977; Heffernan and Lovely, 1991). Other empirical analyses, however, state that officers are in some way deterred (e.g., Orfield, 1987; Uchida and Bynum, 1991; Columbia Law School, 1968; Loewenthal, 1980; Canon, 1979). Thus, the issue of whether the exclusionary rule deters police officers is unclear, at best. The current work will demonstrate that police officers generally do work within legal parameters. Nevertheless, it also shows that there is a need for police departments as well as outside oversight bodies (e.g., civilian complaint review agencies, media, courts, legislatures, etc.) to be ever vigilant.

We now turn to presenting information about the New York City Police Department (NYPD) to determine to what extent, if at all, police officers are constrained by legal guidelines. That is, do police officers feel constrained by the law? The focus will be on typical stop and search activity conducted by officers. Through extensive analyses of these behaviors by police, assessments can be made with respect to these questions.

RESPONSE BY POLICE TO ILLEGAL SITUATIONS

One way to demonstrate the extent of the influence of the law on police officers is to examine how officers are likely to behave in illegal situations. If officers are properly following legal restrictions imposed by the courts, then, when presented with illegal situations, they should choose not to do the behavior asked about (e.g., stop or search). There were three clearly illegal situations presented to police officers in the questionnaire: weapon, marijuana, and car stop situations. Since, at this point, we are looking exclusively at illegal situations, we expect that if officers are obeying the law, they should elect not to do a behavior. That is, police officers in the weapon and marijuana situations should not search, and in the car stop situation they should not conduct the stop. Let's examine each situation individually.

Weapon Situation

As stated, the weapon situation is based on a New York State case, *People v. Jackson* (1992). In the illegal scenario, a driver leaves a locked, double-parked car and casually walks toward an apartment building to ring a doorbell. The officer, on a foot post, is walking near the car. At this point, the officer sees the outline of what could be a gun under a brown paper bag. Since the outline could be almost anything (e.g., a toy or other object), the officer does not yet have the authority to enter the car to determine if it is a gun. The person is within walking distance of the car but plainly far enough away not to be able to grab for the gun. Since the person is not a suspect, is completely out of the vehicle, and is not even remotely able to grab the gun, it is clearly not permissible for officers to conduct a search of the vehicle. Furthermore, the person has made no furtive movements and is "casually walking to an apartment to ring a doorbell." Per the New York State courts, such a scenario outlines a situation in which officers do not yet have the legal authority to search the vehicle. Officers were asked whether, at this point, they would try to retrieve the gun (if it is a gun).

How did police officers respond to this situation? There were **923** responses by New York City officers to this illegal scenario. Of them, **485**

(52.5 percent) stated they were very likely not to search, 290 (31.4 percent) were indecisive about their behavior, and 148 (16 percent) would search. Based on previous research that suggests officers are *most* likely to conduct an illegal search in weapon and drug situations (see especially Heffernan and Lovely, 1991; Nardulli, 1993), we would expect that more than 16 percent would search. Additionally, since the scenario does consist of basically nonegregious illegal behavior that is essentially unsupervised and has very low visibility, one would think that many more officers would search. However, officers in New York City overwhelmingly would not search the car. Unquestionably, officers appear to be influenced by the law in the clearly illegal weapon situation.

Marijuana (Drug) Situation

The marijuana situation is based on another New York State case, *People v. Gokey.* For the illegal scenario, the officer encounters a person, never seen before, who places one hundred marijuana cigarettes into a briefcase and locks the case. The suspect is arrested with several other officers present. There is no key for the briefcase, which is on the ground between the subject's legs. Officers are asked whether they would force open the briefcase at this time. Under these circumstances, officers in New York do not have the power to search the briefcase. This is because the suspect is not a known drug dealer, the briefcase is locked and no key is available, the case is on the ground between the suspect's legs and is not being carried, several other officers are present, and the crime committed is a very minor (i.e., possession of a small amount of marijuana). Officers may, however, arrest the individual and seize the briefcase. To open it at this point and under these circumstances, they must get a search warrant.

What do you suppose police did in this situation? Again, somewhat surprisingly, officers tended to follow legal restrictions. I say "surprisingly" because past research tends to show that officers are most likely to act in an illegal manner in drug and gun situations. Additionally, this is hidden and unsupervised behavior, as well as essentially non-egregious illegal behavior, on the part of officers. There were a total of 910 responses to this question. In this situation 503 (55.3 percent) responses indicated officers would choose not to search, 269 (29.6 percent) responses showed officers were unsure of their behavior, and the remaining 138 (15.2 percent) indicated they would certainly search.

This is a pattern similar to the previous scenario. In fact, a higher percentage of officers would not search in this situation. Again, the majority of officers chose not to search, a smaller number were unsure, and the fewest chose to search. The tendency is clear: officers tend not to search in the gun or marijuana situations.

Car Stop

The car stop situation is based on a United States Supreme Court case, *Delaware v. Prouse*. This case makes it illegal for police officers to stop a car, without any suspicion of illegal activity, to check a driver's license and car registration.[5] The situation, therefore, asks whether the officer would stop the vehicle simply to check the person's operator's license and registration, an illegal act per *Prouse*.

There were 1,252 responses to this situation. Again, the majority of officers chose not to search (623 [49.8 percent]). Next were those who were somewhat unsure of how they would respond (447 [35.7 percent]).[6] The smallest category was officers who would violate the law, and search (182 [14.5 percent]).

Again, the pattern of responses is unmistakable and very similar to the previous two scenarios. That is, there is a tendency for officers not to search in these illegal situations. In this car stop situation, however, officers seemed a little bit less decisive. This is evident from the slight increase in the unsure category. Overall, however, the results are consistent with the previous two scenarios, indicating that officers tend to follow legal parameters even in low visibility, low supervision, nonegregious illegal situations.

INTRODUCTORY IMPLICATIONS AND
SOME RECOMMENDATIONS

In all three situations, approximately 15 percent of police officers stated they would unequivocally do the illegal behavior.[7] Thus, regardless of the situation, when the scenario was illegal, very few officers were disposed to unhesitatingly do the illegal act. Further, in each of the illegal situations, nearly half stated unequivocally that they would *not* do the search or the stop. Although 15 percent of officers would do the illegal behavior in these situations, we must consider that these situations are rarely supervised, are generally out of public view, and are not considered egregious violations of the law.

These findings, then, show that officers clearly *tend* to work within legal parameters. Since we are not studying egregious forms of illegal behavior, but relatively lesser forms of misconduct that would generally be punished through exclusion, civil penalties, and civilian complaints (which could lead to department discipline [generally loss of vacation days]), the finding that officers are generally working within these guidelines is particularly meaningful.[8]

Another reason for these findings being worthwhile is that this information comes from examining behavior that is characteristic of common police activity. These scenarios (car stop, searching a bag, and searching a car) represent typical officer behavior, especially when compared to the more popular research topics in this area, such as studies on the arrest/ no arrest decision. Indeed, some officers work for months or longer without making an arrest.

Bayley (1994: 23) states, "Most of the incidents to which patrol officers respond are routine and undramatic." This study, in particular, shows that in those legal situations which are more commonplace, yet less observed (e.g., search and seizure, stop and frisk), the law is indeed circumscribing officer behavior. Also, the arrest decision tends to be carefully examined by supervisors, watchdog agencies, other officers, the media, and other law enforcement agencies. Although certain violations of the law of search and seizure or stop and frisk will also be scrutinized, such violations are rarely brought to the attention of people in authority. In fact, such incidents generally are not even put on a written record. This is important because police officers generally work with little or no *direct* supervision. Since the situations in the current study are more commonplace, yet less observed, the evidence indicating that the law circumscribes officer behavior in these particular circumstances takes on added importance.

Crime Control Versus Due Process

The finding that police are basically working within legal guidelines is also significant because these incidents are from the *proactive* or *crime control* model of policing that the New York City Police Department is promoting. Many police departments in the United States and elsewhere follow the New York City Police Department's example (see especially Bayley, 1994). Numerous other police agencies are emulating the quality of life crackdown (or zero tolerance, as it is sometimes called), especially the Compstat process (see especially Silverman, 1999).

Given all this interest in the New York City Police Department, it is certainly critical to determine whether or not officers are working within legal restrictions. A focus on the crime control model of policing may lead to increases in abuse of authority (see especially Packer, 1966). Such a model might be expected to increase illegal searches and stops by officers. However, as the data indicate, officers are generally working within legal parameters. Thus, this research shows that it is possible for a police department to focus on crime control while generally maintaining respect for due process.

Finding the proper balance between the crime control and the due process models is a challenge to police administrators. It is critically important to note that those administrators who are attempting to replicate the Compstat (quality of life/zero tolerance model) process in other jurisdictions not only should consider the crime control policies but also should replicate those policies that promote due process (e.g., NYPD *Legal Bureau Bulletins*).

Implications of Current Findings on Limited Versus Unlimited Debate

Unequivocally, the position that we live in a police state is not supported by these initial results. This study shows that the due process protections of law (even at the street level, for legal restrictions that generally do not have strict penalties if they are violated) tend to be reflected in the behavior of frontline practitioners. The data indicate that for precisely those situations where we would expect the greatest amount of police abuse (i.e., basically hidden, unrecorded, and unsupervised activities [also drug and weapon searches]), the majority of officers are following the guidelines and very few officers are outright flouting those restrictions. Thus, this study supports the conclusion that police officers are, in general, obeying due process legal restrictions.

Judicial Impact

Police officers seem to be influenced by search and seizure law. This finding does not with certainty indicate that the remedy of exclusion has had a deterrent effect. That is, the evidence here does not precisely indicate that the exclusionary rule itself is preventing officers from conducting illegal activities. However, it is undeniable that the case law in this area is, at least to some extent, influencing police street behavior. The rulings used for this study were clearly promulgated by the courts in an effort to influence police. The court cases utilized—which have ostensibly been decided on Fourth Amendment grounds (and the equivalent in the New York State Constitution)—have been shown to influence officer behavior. This finding, then, suggests that well known and often cited anecdotal literature which has, at a minimum, hinted that police officers do not feel constrained by such laws (see, for example, Bittner, 1970; Manning, 1977; Skolnick, 1966; Skolnick and Fyfe, 1993; Westley, 1970; Dershowitz, 1996; Davis, 1975; Chevigny, 1969), may not accurately reflect the current state of policing, at least in New York City.

Historical and legal literature on the subject, which tends to suggest that police are somewhat constrained by legal guidelines, seems to portray police more correctly (see, e.g., Kelly et al., 1983; Nevins and

Commager, 1986; Johnson and Canon, 1984). Furthermore, there is some empirical work which suggests that a good number of officers are working within legal constraints. Although these empirical works are clearly aimed at studying general police behavior, they do touch on how officers respond to legal restrictions. In particular, research on officer typologies (i.e., placing officers into categories) shows that certain types of officers are likely to *follow legal restrictions*. In summarizing the literature in this area, Worden points out that at least some officers are likely to follow legal restrictions. Worden (1992a: 19–20) writes:

> *The stereotypical police officer chafes under due process provisions in the single-minded pursuit of criminal offenders, and bitterly resents legal and departmental restrictions concerning search and seizure* . . . but [studies] . . . suggest that cynical officers—such as tough cops and clean-beat crime-fighters—resent legal restrictions on police practices and are willing to violate legal and departmental injunctions when they conflict with the goal of crime control, while other police officers—*professionals and problem-solvers—are willing to work within legal restrictions* (even if they do not applaud them) and may not even feel unnecessarily constrained by them. (Italics added)

A substantial portion of anecdotal literature about the police seems to have seized upon the stereotypical image that Worden (1992a) speaks of. Based on the initial findings presented here, this stereotypical image certainly misrepresents police officers in the United States.

Cause for Concern

Yet there is evidence here to suggest that we need to be cautious. While these findings show that officers in general are following legal restrictions, there was a group of officers, about 15 percent, who were outright willing to violate these legal parameters.[9] This is a cause for concern. At a minimum, it is an indication that officers need to be carefully monitored. Any lawlessness on the part of police officers is unacceptable. The need for police departments themselves, as well as other groups, to be constantly vigilant in overseeing the authority of police is unquestionably indicated. Constant training on these issues to update and reinforce lawful behavior would seem to be a prudent step. Based on some of the comments by officers on the survey, search and seizure training should be coupled with tactical training to help officers understand how the cases are to be handled in the field.

Training is extremely important. Other research has also suggested that the impact of training is critical (e.g., Heffernan and Lovely, 1991). In particular, at the outset of an officer's career, it is essential for the recruit to understand the full ramifications of the law enforcement officer's role. Perhaps some officers do not understand, or fully appreciate, the democratic principles that give them their power and, more important, restrict their power. Police departments, in general, tend to train officers to handle practical situations rather than history and theory. New York City has been moving in that direction. For example, Krauss (1995b: 45) reports that "The New York City Police Department has instituted a new training program in which lecture time on the history of constitutional law and the appeals court process has been slashed and replaced with subjects considered more relevant, like interrogation techniques."

While I agree that practical application is critical, I also feel that— *especially at entry level*—it is equally important for officers to understand their role in the democratic process. Although this is an issue of pedagogy, an understanding of the theoretical basis for an action can assist in practical application. That is, officers who understand *why* they are being told to do something may be more likely to follow directions. Regarding legal restrictions, officers must determine for themselves, in most situations (due to, for example, ambiguous laws and the lack of direct supervision), where to draw the line. Fundamental lessons in history, law, and ethics will assist them in making such a decision. Perhaps this could be taught in a way that demonstrates its practical importance.

After officers graduate and work on the streets, they should be advised of the specific reasons why evidence was excluded at court. Orfield (1987: 1037) states, "Although the officers uniformly believed training was important in understanding the law, they also believed that the lessons of training did not firmly take hold until the officers faced real-life situations in the courtroom." Without constant reinforcement by judges, district attorneys, and in-service training, these lessons may not be fully appreciated or grasped by some street officers. Police today often do not know the outcome of a case due to plea bargaining or dismissal because of legal technicalities that takes place without the officer being present. While this certainly saves time, there is a need for other parts of the criminal justice system to communicate to officers pertinent information such as why a defendant was released (e.g., a bad search because . . .). Something as simple as a letter might suffice; a computer link would be even better. The capabilities are certainly there. It is merely a matter of better linking the different agencies involved. Thus, theory, history, and ethics, as well as practical enforcement, need to be stressed at the Police Academy and constantly reinforced thereafter to prevent police abuse of their lawful authority.

SUMMARY

The impact of courts on police has been the subject of scant scientific inquiry. Ascertaining this impact, however, is of great importance since it has implications for the very heart of our system of government. In a specially designed questionnaire, police officers responded to hypothetical illegal situations. Their responses indicate that the majority of officers unequivocally will not violate legal guidelines. This was true regardless of the situation the officer was placed in. This means that officers generally are following courts' guidelines in typical policing activities. In New York City, in a political climate stressing crime control, most officers are still working within restrictions. This has implications supporting the conclusion that police are not unlimited in their power and that the judiciary is impacting police street behavior. However, there is also cause for concern in that approximately 15 percent were outright violating legal guidelines. This suggests the need for police departments to be ever vigilant with training and programs aimed at supporting legal restrictions.

NOTES

1. As will be discussed, not every part of the Bill of Rights applies to the states. Also, state courts can add to the rights given by the United States Supreme Court (by interpreting their own state constitutions differently), but can never take away that minimum level. These issues add to the confusion law enforcement faces in determining what rules they are required to follow.

2. However, Spiotto seems to have been aware of this problem. He apparently chose to ignore it (see Spiotto, 1973: 246, ftn. 21).

3. In this study, I was vigilant in staying abreast of legal developments to ensure that federal, state, or local law did not adversely impact the research. This was accomplished by getting updates of all laws in New York State, such as the Penal Law and Criminal Procedure Law, as well as consulting the New York State Criminal Law Review Case Notes. United States Supreme Court cases also were followed to ensure that they did not influence the study. As a final check, the New York City Police Department's Legal Bureau and the Police Academy's Management Training Section assisted in updating me on all pertinent changes in the law.

4. It is unknown whether they checked state case law to determine if the courts in each of the seven jurisdictions used their state constitutions to reject *Leon* (1984; the good-faith exception) in that state. Since we do not know the state(s) used, it is impossible to determine this based on the information given.

5. There are situations where police officers can stop cars without suspicion, using authorized checkpoints (e.g., DWI checkpoints). At these checkpoints, however, officers must follow strict guidelines.

6. Given the high percentage of unsure officers, one might think that if the unsure category was skewed toward the illegal end, then nearly 50 percent of officers could be doing the illegal stop. However, further examination of the responses as a simple dichotomy (categorizing officers as either choosing not to do the stop [responded 1–4] or choosing to do the illegal stop [responded 5–8]), we see that 68.6 percent of officers chose not to do the stop while only 31.4 percent chose to do the stop.

7. Heffernan and Lovely (1991) show similar percentages but interpret their results to mean the law is too complicated in this area for officers to be deterred. I will discuss this ambiguity in the law in another chapter. Nevertheless, it appears that officers are being deterred by the restrictions where the situation presented to them is clearly outside legal parameters.

8. However, as stated earlier, officers have been arrested for illegal searches. Furthermore, department discipline can result in the loss of the job. However, arrest and the loss of the job are extremely unusual penalties for violating such restrictions.

9. There were 138 drug and 148 weapon vignettes with illegal responses. Of these, a total of twenty-two drug and twenty-seven weapon situations were from a respondent who received more than one illegal scenario. This means 116 and 121 subjects responded illegally to the drug and weapon scenarios, respectively. Of these, sixteen responded illegally to both.

CHAPTER 4

The Impact on Police of Ambiguity in the Law

Basic statistics have been used to demonstrate that the law does indeed have an impact on police behavior. This issue, however, is exceedingly complicated. One aspect of this complexity is that the judiciary, in trying to enforce the Fourth Amendment (and its parallel in state constitutions) on police through the exclusionary rule, has created a very elaborate and convoluted body of law. Due to this ambiguity written into the law by the courts, it only seems logical to deduce that there is equally ambiguous guidance for police. In describing this matter at the federal level, Israel and LaFave (1988: 2) write:

> Almost every Supreme Court term has been marked by several decisions producing significant new developments in constitutional criminal procedure, and by a larger group of rulings that fine tuned previously announced standards. As a result, every major stage of the criminal justice process is today subject to significant constitutional standards developed in decisions in the past thirty years. Moreover, some basic elements of the process (e.g., police searches) are now subject to constitutional regulations, developed in a lengthy series of Supreme Court rulings, so extensive that they rival the most complex statutory codes in their comprehensiveness and intricacy.

IMPORTANT COMMENTARY ON AMBIGUITY IN THE LAW

There is one topic on which almost every writer on the law and police agrees: that there is a lack of clarity in Fourth Amendment law. Authors overwhelmingly feel that these laws are especially complicated and not intelligible. Indeed, they often speak of the puzzling array of legal jargon expressed in Fourth Amendment judicial interpretation. Justices, researchers, law enforcement officers, and other experts in the field are practically unanimous in their critiques. Let's examine some of these works.

Judge Harold Rothwax (1996: 40–41), who served on the New York State Supreme Court, elaborated on this issue:

> The problem is, the law is so muddy that the police can't find out what they are allowed to do even if they wanted to. If a street cop took a sabbatical and holed himself up in a library for six months doing nothing but studying the law on search and seizure, he wouldn't know any more than he did before he started. The law is totally confusing, yet we expect cops to always know at every moment what the proper action is. It's no wonder that police officers are somewhat edgy—especially when they're pursuing cases involving vicious murderers and rapists.

The new officer, in particular, is filled with uncertainties about how to handle situations. On the one hand, the rookie has been given numerous legal rules; on the other hand are the realities of street enforcement. As Herman Goldstein (1977: 101) writes:

> What typically happens is that officers discover, upon graduating from their recruit training and taking their first assignments, that they are constantly being called upon to make decisions; that relatively little of what they were taught seems to apply to the situations they confront; and that they are often without guidance in deciding what to do in a given situation. They gradually learn, from their association with more experienced personnel and from their supervisors, that there is a mass of "know-how" upon which they must draw. Practices, they find, vary a great deal. Some seem so well established that they take on the quality of a standard departmental operating procedure utilized uniformly by all personnel. Though these may not have any legal basis (some may, in fact, be clearly illegal) and are not formally recognized, they are employed so routinely that reference to them commonly creeps into departmental reports and forms.

Some commentators go so far as to say that the Supreme Court is shirking its responsibility when a particular opinion is so unclear as to confuse those who must follow its rulings more than if the issue had not been brought before the Court. For example, Joseph Goldstein (1992: 8) writes:

> The Court's task must be to make comprehensible provisions of the Constitution whose language has conveyed different meanings to different minds. This should not obscure the fact that the language of opinions may

be no more free of ambiguity than the language of the constitutional provisions. Nevertheless, the Court's task of explaining, of giving reasons for its judgment in a concrete case, is to clarify—to make something about the Constitution more fully understood than it was before the opinion was rendered.

Wayne LaFave, one of the most respected Fourth Amendment scholars, speaks of this area of the law as being cumbersome. To get his point across he quotes Justice Tom Campbell Clark in *Chapman v. United States* (1961), who wrote (LaFave, 1972: 9–10):

> Every moment of every day, somewhere in the United States, a law enforcement officer is faced with the problem of search and seizure. He is anxious to obey the rules that circumscribe his conduct in the field. It is the duty of the Court to lay down those rules with such clarity and understanding that he may be able to follow them. For some years now the field has been muddy, but today the Court makes it a quagmire.

LaFave quotes Justice Clark to emphasize the image of a "quagmire" to describe Fourth Amendment law. LaFave (1972: 30) continues, "Finally, it is not inappropriate to suggest that the rules governing search and seizure, including when a warrant is required, are more in need of greater clarity than greater sophistication."

Over the years many other respected legal experts have stated that Fourth Amendment law is very unclear. Dworkin (1973: 333–334) writes, "Fourth amendment law is so uncertain, incomprehensible, quibble ridden, and ever changing that it deprives any sanction of a meaningful chance to control conduct." Kamisar (1990: 557), a staunch defender of the exclusionary rule, states, "The rule only made a *difficult and complex* body of law relevant" (italics added). Amsterdam (1974: 349) writes, "For clarity and consistency, the law of the Fourth Amendment is not the Supreme Court's most successful product." According to Baum (1985: 204), "Decisions that are inconsistent with each other in spirit create ambiguity. . . . This is true of the Court's decisions on police procedure." Others could easily be cited here as well (see especially Grano, 1982: 603; Canon, 1979: 399; and Oaks, 1970: 731). Recent periodical literature has blasted the courts on this issue. Reinharz (1996: 45–46), writing for the *City Journal*, specifically discusses New York's Court of Appeals: "Street encounters between police and suspects is a prime area in which the Court of Appeals has swept aside the commonsense judgment of cops and erected instead an absurd, hopelessly confusing framework of legal rules."[1]

EXPLAINING AMBIGUITY IN THE LAW

Obviously, many scholars believe Fourth Amendment law is ambiguous. What is this ambiguity? Where does it come from? Interestingly, a lack of clarity in the law is partially a symptom of the wording of the Constitution, including the Bill of Rights. It is possible that the founding fathers purposely left certain passages somewhat unclear to allow the law to bend with the times (see especially Nevins and Commager, 1986; Kelly et al., 1983; and Nardulli, 1992). This, however, leads to an unavoidable tension during periods where there is a lack of societal consensus on a particular issue. Nardulli (1992: 5), for example, writes:

> A certain level of ambiguity in a document such as a constitution is unavoidable and to some extent desirable. The ambiguity of key provisions of the U.S. Constitution has permitted it to breathe with history and undoubtedly accounts for its longevity, but it is the same ambiguity that obscures the Constitution's role in American political development.

Ambiguity in the Constitution, then, can be seen as both a blessing and a curse. The blessing is the Constitution's flexibility to change with the times. The curse is an inability to understand its meaning.

Certain aspects of the Civil War in the United States provide us with a real-life example of the possible deleterious effects of interpreting ambiguous constitutional provisions. The problem of slavery came to a peak in the late 1850s. The Constitution was unclear on several matters related to this. Certain issues had to be explained clearly. Some states had slavery, but others did not. How were runaway slaves to be handled by states that did not have slavery? Could new states have slaves? Constitutional law was unclear; the states needed guidance. Eventually the Supreme Court decided one of the most controversial cases in United States history, *Dred Scott v. Sanford* (1857). The Court, under Chief Justice Roger Taney, held that blacks were not citizens under the Constitution, and therefore could not sue in the federal courts. Additionally, the Court held that the Missouri Compromise, which was an attempt by the Congress to deal with the controversial issue of slavery, was unconstitutional. The Court also held that Missouri law was binding on Scott, who now lived there. This meant that Scott, who for a time lived in territory considered free by the Compromise, was still a slave.

This decision attempted to clarify a matter *purposely left vague* by our founding fathers: the issues of slavery and states' rights (i.e., federalism). The Supreme Court's decision was so unpopular in the North that it was unenforceable, and it is likely that it contributed to the outbreak of war (see especially Kelly et al., 1983: 254, 271, 298).

Nevertheless, it does seem that if a court wants to, it can eliminate much ambiguity. As Johnson and Canon (1984: 204–205) write:

> *Roe v. Wade* (1973) lays down specific rules as to what regulation of abortion was allowable, and this specificity undoubtedly helped to improve implementation of the decision. . . . In legislative apportionment the Court established a somewhat vague principle of equality in district population, but it then decided a large number of additional cases to clarify the application of that principle. As a result, lower court judges learned what was expected of them and could follow through. *These two areas underline the capacity of a determined Court to reduce the ambiguity of its policies and thereby improve their implementation.* (Italics added)

Courts, then, may purposely leave a decision vague. This may be to allow for flexibility. Another possibility is that a compromise on wording may be necessary to achieve unanimity or even a majority. This may have been the situation, for example, in the Supreme Court case *Brown v. Board of Education of Topeka* (1955).[2] Using the words "with all deliberate speed" (rather than, say, "immediately" or "as soon as possible") certainly leaves room for interpretation. In fact, in writing about this decision Segal and Spaeth (1993: 344) state, "No wonder that a decade elapsed before any appreciable changes occurred in the Deep South . . . the blame should at least partially fall on the occupants of the Marble Palace." This blame, they argue, is due to the ambiguous language of the Court.

To help shed light on the issue of vague court decisions, an understanding of the basic theories about how courts arrive at their decisions is helpful. There are essentially two schools of thought as to how legal decisions are arrived at. Segal and Spaeth describe these two schools: "[The] . . . *legal model* that we describe and critique has four variants that the justices themselves employ: plain meaning, intent of the framers (or legislators), precedent, and balancing . . . , [whereas the *attitudinal model* is that Supreme Court decisions are based on the] attitudes and values of the justices" (Segal and Spaeth, 1993: i, 33).

Under the legal model it is argued that it is critical to understand the framers' intent. Many comments have been made regarding the Fourth Amendment's original meaning. Bradford Wilson (1983: 183) states, "This is not to say, however, that the fourth amendment gives fixed constitutional status to any one remedy. . . . The point to be emphasized is that the Framers did not regard the fourth amendment as impotent." Grano (1982) goes through an entire history of searches and suggests that the framers wanted to constrict the power of the executive or they would not have drafted the Amendment. Grano (1982: 620) argues that the framers wanted to express grievances in general terms intended to endure beyond their own lifetimes. Relating this to police work, Amsterdam (1974: 414–415) writes, "The view prevails that the Framers of the Fourth Amendment have given us only the *general* standard of 'unreasonableness' as a guide in determining whether searches and seizures meet the standard of the Amendment in those cases where a warrant is not required, and the 'unreasonableness' standard is obviously *much too amorphous* either to guide or to regulate the police" (Italics added).

As modern jurisprudence attempts to interpret the Fourth Amendment, it is difficult to know what was meant or, indeed, if the issue of a case could have meant anything to those who wrote it. For example, the Supreme Court case *Florida v. Riley* (1989) held that the Fourth Amendment was not violated by a police officer who saw drug plants in a greenhouse while in a helicopter that was four hundred feet above the property. The Court reasoned that a person does not have a "reasonable expectation of privacy" in such circumstances, since the helicopter was in a place where any member of the public could legally be. The use of a helicopter obviously would have been impossible at the time the amendment was written. The meaning of the Fourth Amendment, in this case, was extremely uncertain, partially because the framers had no conception of modern technology.

Others argue that ambiguity has helped the police. Atkinson (1985: 263–264), for example, states:

> Search and seizure law has moved unmistakably during the past several years toward an increased acceptance of police decision making in situations where warrants have not been issued by neutral magistrates based on probable cause. The police increasingly have been allowed to act on their own assessment of probable cause. . . . What accounts for the Court's willingness to be even more deferential to police judgements reached in the field as to what is constitutionally appropriate? One answer may lie with the vagueness of the Fourth Amendment. . . . Another factor in the Court's recent decisions may be its perception of the extent of the seriousness and extent of contemporary crime.

Additionally, as Atkinson (1985) and Segal and Spaeth (1993) argue, the attitudes or points of view of the membership of the Court are swaying these decisions. The current prevailing view of the United States Supreme Court is likely to be favorable to police. The Supreme Court is more conservative, and therefore the police are more likely to receive favorable decisions.[3] One case that demonstrates how the Court has deferred to the police is *Colorado v. Bertine* (1987).

In this decision, the Supreme Court held that as long as the police are conducting an inventory search according to standardized department procedures, and are not using the inventory search as a ruse to discover evidence (i.e., they are acting in good faith), the search will withstand constitutional muster. However, other United States Supreme Court cases can be cited that do not support this pro-police position, such as *Florida v. J.L.* (2000) (an anonymous tip that a person is carrying a gun is not, without more evidence, sufficient to justify a police officer's stop and frisk) or *Illinois v. Wardlow* (2000) (unprovoked flight upon seeing police is not, of itself, reasonable suspicion, meaning a police officer does not have the power to forcibly stop such a fleeing person).

NEW YORK STATE COURTS

Although the United States Supreme Court has been sharply criticized for its lack of clarity regarding Fourth Amendment law, it can be argued that the highest Court has issued relatively clear rulings compared to the New York State Court of Appeals. For example, in the case of *New York v. Belton* (1981), the United States Supreme Court held that a search incident to a lawful arrest of a person in an auto includes the entire passenger compartment of the vehicle as well as contents of containers, whether closed or open, locked or unlocked. The Court explicitly decided this case with the expressed purpose of constructing an understandable bright-line rule for police (i.e., lawful arrest equals search of the passenger compartment).

In contrast, the New York State Court of Appeals (the highest court in New York) under the New York Constitution has interpreted the law in a less coherent manner. The Court of Appeals ruled in *People v. Galak* (1993) that a police officer may conduct a warrantless search of an automobile after arresting the occupant only if the officer has probable cause to believe that the vehicle contains evidence or contraband *and* there is a nexus between the probable cause to search and the crime for which the arrest is being made. Thus, in New York, if a police officer is not making an arrest, all that is needed is probable cause to search a vehicle (see *United States v. Ross* [1982]); however, if a police officer is making an arrest, the officer needs more than probable cause to search the vehicle. That is, you need probable cause *plus* a nexus between the probable cause to search and the crime for which the arrest is being made. Confused? Well, so is everyone else.

State courts have complicated matters by creating a parallel body of law based on state constitutions.[4] In New York, the Court of Appeals, in particular, has interpreted the New York State Constitution in such a way as to make its intent exceedingly difficult to understand. In fact, policing advocates have often claimed that the New York courts are particularly hostile to law enforcement. For example, according to the *New York Times* (Levy, 1996: 1), "Governor George E. Pataki went on the attack against the state's highest court. [He introduced legislation] which would essentially loosen the rules that the authorities must follow in searching and seizing evidence from criminal suspects."

Former New York City Police Commissioner William Bratton also argues that the New York State courts are particularly unclear, and even show animosity toward police. He summed up what he believes to be the anti-police position of the New York courts while sharing a platform with seven influential judges and lawyers, stating (cited in Haberman, 1996: B1), "Let New York courts operate under more police-friendly rules laid down by the United States Supreme Court rather than the screwball system that we have in this state with the screwball Court of Appeals. . . . I think all of us are in agreement that we have a Court of Appeals that is just living off in Disneyworld somewhere. They're not living in the streets of New York."

Richard D. Simmons, a retired New York State Court of Appeals judge, defended the position of the court, stating (cited in Dao, 1996: B28), "We're not part of the executive branch. We're not on the team with the police to catch criminals. We're referees to make sure the police and courts have obeyed the rules and that defendants have gotten fair trials and the guarantees the constitution gives them. Unfortunately, some people think it is our job to put people in jail or prosecute them."

As demonstrated, court decisions regarding search and seizure law, especially in New York, are often extremely unclear. They give little, if any, guidance to the police or to lower courts. If we accept the hypotheses of Atkinson (1985) and of Segal and Spaeth (1993), this lack of clarity may be due to the point of view of the state court justices. That is, there may be a reluctance of the more liberal members on the New York State court to accept the more conservative Supreme Court's interpretation (often said to be written with more clarity compared to New York court decisions). Interestingly, it has even been suggested that the United States Supreme Court is particularly susceptible to shifts in membership on this issue (see especially Atkinson, 1985: 266). Each time a new member is appointed to the Court, it is likely that a shift in Fourth Amendment interpretation will occur making it even more difficult to follow the law's guidelines.

Surprisingly little empirical inquiry has examined the impact of these controversial New York State courts' decisions. In fact, scant research has been conducted on the impact of any state court. For example, Johnson and Canon (1984: 237) point out that "The fact is that virtually no one has studied the policy impact of state supreme courts."[5] This chapter will focus on explaining the impact of a lack of clarity in written court decisions on frontline practitioners, including the impact of a state court.

BRIGHT-LINE RULES

This discussion on ambiguity in the law leads to a related point. It has been suggested that the solution to this lack of clarity is for courts to write their decisions in bright-line rules. In fact, many experts in this area argue that bright-line rules (i.e., straightforward, easily applied guidelines rather than case-by-case analyses) are needed to make sense of (and perhaps increase compliance with) the incomprehensible laws on search and seizure (e.g., Amsterdam, 1974; Baum, 1985; Butterfoss, 1988; J. Goldstein, 1984; Grano, 1982; O'Brien, 1993; Reinharz, 1996, Whitebread, 1985). They basically feel that, to the extent possible, rules need to be explicated so as to guide frontline practitioners who are attempting to adhere to court decisions. For example, Whitebread (1985: 472) states, "I feel quite fervently the imperative of rule-oriented decision-making in police related cases. It is a major jurisprudential error . . . to leave the police uncertain as to what they may lawfully do. . . . Without clear rules, the police will have no reliable idea of what they may do, many mistakes will be made and, if we use exclusion, guilty people will go unpunished because of police mistakes."

Many authors feel that the impact of ambiguity in a court's decision leads to erratic enforcement. There are many examples of this throughout the literature. Joseph Goldstein (1992: 19, 115) writes:

> Whether the justices be activists or passivists, they have a professional obligation to articulate in comprehensible and accessible language the constitutional principles on which their judgments rest. . . . That the Constitution be intelligible and accessible to We the People of the United States is requisite to a government by consent; a government that guarantees equal protection and due process of the law. . . . If they do not speak with candor and clarity in their opinions, they will deprive Us, the governed, of the capacity to know what the law does and does not require, and thus exclude Us from the opportunity to participate fully in government. Likewise, they will deprive governors (who are also counted among the governed) of guidelines for meeting their constitutional responsibilities.

Sutton (1986) interviewed police officers, who discussed the problem of practicing the law of search and seizure. Sutton (1986: 412) writes, "we heard additional complaints about judicial inconsistencies in interpreting and applying the law on search and seizure." Oaks (1970: 731) argues, "The deterrent effectiveness of the exclusionary rule is also dependent upon whether the arrest and search and seizure rules that it is supposed to enforce are stated with sufficient clarity that they can be understood and followed by common ordinary police officers." Prottas (1978) discusses the impact of ambiguity on the street-level bureaucrat. He states, "For the management of any organization to effectively oversee the behavior of its low-level employees it must (1) define with some clarity what behavior shall be considered proper" (Prottas, 1978: 294). Delattre (1994: 53) writes, "A police officer needs sense of relevant laws . . . problems arise over court rulings of the Fourth Amendment. . . . Their trend [the courts' ambiguity] may increase the discretion of judges in lower courts more than discretionary authority elsewhere. It will not make judgment easier for police in the streets, because it will not make explicit any general guides to conduct." These works certainly suggest that ambiguity in the law will prevent compliance by police officers.

However, Johnson and Canon (1984) suggest that a lack of clarity in the law will not necessarily lead to a measurable decrease in compliance. One reason for this is that, "The greater the ambiguity of the case or the policy, the wider the range of possible interpretations. Ironically, interpretations are also less likely to be noncompliant, since noncompliance is difficult to define for ambiguous decisions or policies" (Johnson and Canon, 1984: 54). Also, Johnson and Canon (1984: 208) state, "While it is reasonable to believe that final, clear, and persuasive decisions receive greater compliance than those lacking such qualities, scattered research indicates otherwise."

There are some, nevertheless, who argue that bright-line rules are not a solution; rather, they feel that giving a *general direction of reasonableness* would be better (e.g., Alschuler, 1984; Rothwax, 1996). That is, actions which the courts decide are reasonable should be considered legal. In any event, both these schools of thought appear to be in basic agreement that something needs to be done about the lack of clarity in the law. Joseph Goldstein (1992: 19) effectively summarizes this when he writes, "There is no expectation that the Court's formulations will ever be fully comprehensible or ambiguity-free. But the goal must be that the Court's interpretations of the Constitution are understandable at their core—that they serve to prevent it from taking on the complexity of a body of regulations."

It can also be argued that bright-line rules favor conservative lawmaking. Thus, if a court is conservative, it could conceivably hide its rightwing intentions by claiming the need to write bright-line rules. Clear and sensible rules, however, also can be drawn up with a liberal focus. For example, a court could write a rule into its decision such as "After an arrest from a vehicle, no search of that vehicle is permissible without a search warrant." Certainly this is liberal, as well as clear and concise. As LaFave (1993: 267) states, "If there are to be some bright lines in police rules, they should not inevitably be drawn as the Supreme Court has been inclined to draw them . . . most intrusive on the interests of privacy and liberty." So while the Supreme Court can be criticized for its lack of clarity in guiding police, when it does write bright-line rules, they are generally conservative (which bright-line rules do not have to be). This should not be unexpected, given the current views of the justices.

It has been demonstrated that the courts have been, in general, extremely ambiguous in their rulings regarding police procedure. This ambiguity allows flexibility but prevents understanding. Given the previous discussion, two issues become apparent and we now turn to them. First, examining the issue of to what extent, if at all, ambiguity influences police officers' behavior in the field. Second, analyzing the question of to what extent, if at all, bright-line rules assist officers in following court rulings.

RESPONSE BY POLICE TO AMBIGUOUSLY WORDED LEGAL SITUATIONS

To examine the influence of ambiguity in the law, the questionnaire administered to New York City police officers is helpful. The questionnaire allows comparison of officers' responses to different types of situations involving ambiguous court decisions. The first way to study the influence of ambiguity is utilizing scenarios from the questionnaire that have two levels of legal ambiguity, slightly ambiguous and highly ambiguous. Scenarios that fit these criteria were constructed using the court cases previously discussed—one for drug situations (*People v. Gokey*) and another for weapon situations *(People v. Jackson)*.

Drug Situations

A slightly ambiguous scenario contains information that leaves the legality of the situation somewhat unclear as to whether officers may search a duffel bag. In this situation, the suspect is a known drug dealer, the duffel bag is on the ground between the suspect's legs and is not being carried by the suspect, and the officer immediately seizes the bag. The legal question officers need to ask is whether or not there is a threat to officer safety or evidence. Since the scenario involves a known drug dealer—and most drug dealers are dangerous—the officer might be able to articulate the need to search the bag. On the other hand, there is no apparent immediate threat to officer safety or the evidence and therefore the officer could merely seize the bag and later obtain a search warrant, similar to the *Gokey* case. Therefore, this situation is slightly ambiguous (legally).

Another situation was created that is even more unclear legally. The suspect is no longer a known drug dealer, the bag is now locked shut (although a key is immediately available), the duffel bag is on the ground between the suspect's legs and is not being carried, other officers are present (lessening the threat), and the officer has already frisked the person without seizing the bag (indicating a lack of a threat from the bag). All these facts taken together leave the situation very unclear as to whether officers could legally search the duffel bag.

Results: Drug Situations

When examining officers' responses to these ambiguous drug situations, we see a clear pattern in which officers are markedly influenced by ambiguity in the legal situation. At the slightly ambiguous level, officers *increased* their search behavior by about 10 percent compared to the unambiguous legal scenario. Specifically, when the situation was unambiguously legal, officers responded that they are sure they would search in 44.2 percent of the situations. When the situation was slightly ambiguous legally, more officers decided to search (53.5 percent). Thus, officers in the drug situations took advantage of the slightly ambiguous situation and searched the bag more often. What happens when the situation becomes extremely unclear legally? Do officers again increase their search activity? The answer is *no*. When the drug situation was highly ambiguous, officers significantly *decreased* their search behavior (38.6 percent). In sum, when the situation is slightly unclear, officers in the drug scenarios take advantage of the ambiguity and search more often; however, when the situation becomes very unclear legally, they tend to search much less.

Weapon Situation

Two legally ambiguous weapon situations were also created. The slightly ambiguous scenario purposely outlines a situation in which it is somewhat unclear as to whether officers might legally be able to enter an automobile in order to conduct a search for a weapon. At this level, the person in the situation does not fit the description of a robbery suspect, is not situated in or out of the car, and what appears to be a gun is "next to the driver's seat." More specifically, as the officer approaches the auto, the driver begins to get out of the vehicle and is standing with one foot on the pavement and the other in the car. The New York court does not address the issue of whether officers may legally search a car when a person is neither fully in nor fully out of the vehicle. This particular fact pattern, therefore, helped make the situation slightly ambiguous. Also, the apparent gun is next to the driver's seat. It is not entirely clear whether the person could immediately grasp it, which is an important aspect of the legal situation since officers can legally search only if the person can immediately grasp the weapon. At this point, with the person neither in nor out of the vehicle and the apparent gun next to the driver's seat, officers must assess the situation.

In the highly ambiguous scenario the situation becomes even more convoluted as to whether it is legally permissible to conduct a search of the auto for the weapon. As in the slightly ambiguous scenario, the person does not fit the description of a robbery suspect and is not situated in or out of the car (one foot on the pavement and the other in the car). However, the weapon is now even further away (i.e., in the rear seat on the passenger side), making it more difficult for the person to get it. The location of the weapon makes it even more ambiguous as to whether officers can legally enter the car to search for the gun.

Results: Weapon Situation

The results from the survey indicate that unlike the drug situations, officers in the weapon scenarios were not significantly influenced by the ambiguous situations. Specifically, officers in the weapon situations tended to search in both ambiguous situations at a rate similar to the legal situation. In all three situations, officers searched about 29 percent of the time. This may be due to the danger posed by the weapon incorporated into this scenario. It seems plausible that in situations which are inherently more dangerous, officers who are willing to search (and there are fewer of them compared to the drug situation—on average 38 percent searched in the drug situations versus 25 percent in the weapon situations, regardless of legality) are more concerned with removing the danger than with violating ambiguous legal restrictions.[6] Thus, some officers may choose to stretch the law to its limits to remove the danger. As James Wilson (1977: 39, 44) states, "The patrolman confronting a citizen is especially alert to two kinds of cues: those that signal danger and those that signal impropriety." However, while officers did tend to search for the weapon in ambiguous situations, in general, they did *not* go so far as to violate legal guidelines.[7] Recall our earlier discussion showing that in the illegal situations, officers searched only about 15 percent of the time. There was, therefore, a significant decrease in officers' search behavior at the illegal level, *but only at the illegal level.* Ambiguity in the law had little impact on officers' search decisions with regard to a weapon. They searched as if it were completely and unambiguously legal to do so.

Bright-Line Versus Ambiguous Cases

A second way to study the influence of ambiguity in the law using the questionnaire is comparing two separate court cases (rather than ambiguity within a case, as was done previously). Two other scenarios based on court cases were created—one based on a bright-line case and another on an ambiguous decision. This dichotomy, bright-line versus non-bright-line, is suggested by numerous authors (e.g., Amsterdam, 1974; Butterfoss, 1988; Heffernan and Lovely, 1991; LaFave, 1993; Reinharz, 1996; Whitebread, 1985). For our purposes, a bright-line case is one that incorporates a clear, sensible rule which apparently offers effective guidance to law enforcement. An ambiguous case is one that apparently offers little guidance to law enforcement, contains at least one important term that is weakly defined, and has a rationale that tends to be weak or even senseless.[8]

The bright-line situation is drawn from the United States Supreme Court Case *Delaware v. Prouse* (1979). The scenario constructed from this case involves stopping a vehicle without any suspicion of illegal activity. The stop is ostensibly being conducted to check the driver's operator's license and the vehicle registration. This is illegal per the *Prouse* decision. Thus, officers are asked whether or not they would stop a car without suspicion—an illegal act.

An ambiguous or non-bright-line scenario is constructed using a New York State Court of Appeals case, *People v. Martinez* (1992). The scenario based on this case involves a person running from an officer who is in full uniform. The person flees merely upon sight of the officer. The respondents are then asked whether they would "*run after*" the suspect. Because the court said it is illegal to pursue, "*running after*" the person definitely is highly questionable behavior and violates the spirit of the decision, but it is not necessarily illegal.

Results: Bright-Line Versus Ambiguous Court Cases

Both scenarios are essentially illegal. (However, for the ambiguous case we cannot definitely say this is so because the decision is so unclear.) Therefore, if the ambiguity of a case is having an influence, we might expect officers to respond by doing the behavior more often in the ambiguous case (running after the person) because they (and many others) do not fully understand the decision.

Indeed, for the bright-line case, officers' judgments tended toward not doing the behavior compared to the ambiguous case. This is supported by comparing the average of the judgments in the two cases. (Officers judged on a scale of 1 to 8, with 1 being definitely not search and 8 being definitely search.) The average of judgments in the bright-line case is 3.32. For the ambiguous case, the average of the judgments was 3.72 (the higher average indicates that officers are stating they would do the activity more often). The average difference in the judgments is 0.40.[9] This is an extremely important difference. It means that officers were significantly more likely to follow the decision in the bright-line case. That is, they were more likely to do the illegal running after the suspect in the ambiguous case compared to stopping the car in the bright-line case.

Other analyses also indicate that officers are more likely to obey the law in responding to the bright-line case scenario. For example, 35 percent of officers responded they definitely would not do the car stop in the bright-line case. Comparing that figure to the ambiguous case, in which only 25 percent of officers stated they definitely would not stop the person, again indicates that officers are responding quite differently to these cases. We see a difference of about 10 percent in the direction supporting the use of bright-line rules. That is, officers tend to do the illegal behavior less often in the bright-line case.

DISCUSSION

In the car/person stop situations (bright-line versus ambiguous legal scenarios), the evidence was clear that officers will respond by doing a behavior less often in illegal situations if the court explicates a rule in clear terms. That is, in the bright-line case officers tended to do the car stop significantly less often compared to the ambiguous person stop case. To help prevent officers from straying beyond the boundaries of the law, the evidence here suggests that clear and concise rulings would seem to help, although not to prevent, the problem of illegal police activity in this area. This supports statements by such authors as Vorenberg (1976: 689), who suggests, "The police investigative practices that have been subjected to judicial scrutiny through application of the exclusionary rule—search and seizure, interrogation and lineups— have already been referred to as examples of the difficulty in case-by-case judicial review as a means of preventing abuse of discretion."

As demonstrated, bright-line rules do help officers stay within courts' guidelines, and could go a long way toward preventing incidents. One such incident that might be prevented was discussed earlier: the arrest and conviction of Lieutenant Patricia Feerick (a New York City police officer convicted and sentenced—later pardoned by the Governor of New York—for conducting an illegal search). Many distinguished scholars have crusaded for more clarity in the law (e.g., Baum, 1985; Grano, 1982; LaFave, 1974; and Whitebread, 1985).

However, there is scant research which suggests that just a few bright-line rules in this area will neither reduce ambiguity nor increase compliance in this area of the law. Heffernan and Lovely (1991), for example, compared the bright-line rules of *Miranda* (Fifth Amendment) with certain search and seizure cases (Fourth Amendment). Based on results from their questionnaire, they argue that limited bright-line rules will not help the situation with search and seizure. Regardless, this book, in comparing two Fourth Amendment cases—one bright-line and the other ambiguous—does suggest that bright-line rules in even one court case will result in increased compliance and, therefore, help the situation (if only slightly). Heffernan and Lovely's (1991) point may, however, be somewhat accurate; that is, courts may need to adopt a philosophy of deciding Fourth Amendment cases in a sensible pattern of bright-line rules before the exceedingly convoluted nature of this area of the law is seriously affected.

The United States Supreme Court has acknowledged the need for bright-line rules. For example, in *California v. Acevedo* (1991), Justice Harry Blackmun wrote for the Court, "We conclude that it is better to adopt one clear-cut rule to govern automobile searches and eliminate the warrant requirement for closed containers." In *Dunaway v. New York* (1979), Justice William Brennan wrote for the Court, "A single, familiar standard is essential to guide police officers, who have only limited time and expertise to reflect on and balance the social and individual interests involved in the specific circumstances they confront." The Supreme Court in *New York v. Belton* (1981) quoted LaFave (1974), which effectively summarizes this argument:

> Fourth Amendment doctrine, given force and effect by the exclusionary rule, is primarily intended to regulate the police in their day-to-day activities and thus ought to be expressed in terms that are readily applicable by the police in the context of the law enforcement activities in which they are necessarily engaged. A highly sophisticated set of rules, qualified by all sorts of ifs, ands, and buts and requiring the drawing of subtle nuances and hairline distinctions, may be the sort of heady stuff upon which the facile minds of lawyers and judges eagerly feed, but they may be literally impossible of application by the officer in the field.

However, the United State Supreme Court in *Illinois v. Wardlow* (2000) rejected the bright-line argument *made by both parties in the case!* Perhaps the intent of the current Court is to allow ambiguity for the sake of flexibility, since they themselves are unsure where to draw an appropriate balance. This does give police some leeway. The evidence indicates that officers did take advantage of this ambiguity in both the weapon and drug situations.

Nevertheless, a lack of guidance from the courts leaves police officers in a very precarious position and, in fact, may be an attempt by courts to shift responsibility to frontline practitioners. Officers, although somewhat trained in legal restrictions, are not lawyers or judges. Yet, as demonstrated, even lawyers and judges under calm conditions have enormous difficulty with the law of the Fourth Amendment or its counterpart in state constitutions. How do the courts expect officers with limited expertise, and under less than ideal conditions (sometimes under enormous stress, with only seconds to make a decision), to properly execute incomprehensible rulings?

Complicating matters, officers' responses to ambiguity within the same court case seems to vary depending on the level of ambiguity and situational factors. In both the drug and weapon situations, officers took advantage of slight ambiguity to conduct searches (more so in the drug cases). Yet, in the highly ambiguous situations officers decreased their search intensity in the drug scenarios but searched at a similar rate as the legal situation in the weapon scenarios. This may be due to the danger officers associate with weapons. We can conclude that ambiguity in a court's decision has an influence on officers' behavior. All things being equal, bright-line decisions are more likely to be followed by officers. Officers' responses to ambiguity within the same court case seems to vary according to the level of ambiguity and situational factors.

SUMMARY

The impact of the law on police is complicated by ambiguity written into the law by the courts. Fourth Amendment law is especially unclear. This lack of clarity is partially a symptom of the wording of the Constitution. Ambiguity in the law can be both good and bad—good in that it allows some flexibility in the law to change with the times, but bad in that a lack of clarity makes the law difficult to understand. State courts have further complicated matters especially in New York, where a parallel body of law, even more convoluted than at the federal level, was created. Court decisions incorporating bright-line rules (i.e., straightforward, easily applied guidelines) have been suggested by many experts as one way to help alleviate this lack of clarity in Fourth Amendment law. Results from a questionnaire answered by officers in New York City suggest that this ambiguity in courts' decisions does influence police street behavior.

However, the influence of ambiguity seems to depend on two key factors: the level of clarity and the type of situation. Officers take advantage of slight ambiguity in the law regardless of the situation. Yet in dangerous activities it appears that officers will take advantage of ambiguous legal situations and stretch the law to its limits—searching as necessary. Importantly, the survey also indicates that bright-line decisions are more likely to be obeyed by police.

NOTES

1. For another example see Levy (1996: A1).

2. The words "all deliberate speed" were used when the Court determined the remedy of constitutional principles decided in the previous year in *Brown v. Board of Education of Topeka* (1954).

3. However, see Simon (1995) for another point of view.

4. State courts have the power to interpret their state constitutions within the boundaries of the United States Constitution. That is, state courts may give more rights, but never less, than what the Supreme Court states is an acceptable constitutional minimum.

5. This is not to suggest that no work has been accomplished at the state level. Burton et al. (1993), for example, examine all fifty states' legal codes in an attempt to determine tasks required of police. Their interest, however, is in whether laws have been enacted that affect the service function of policing. They do not examine the extent of the impact, if any, this legislation has on law enforcement. Thus, they basically counted and categorized legislative activity. Burton et al. conclude that the service role is defined at the local level.

6. It is difficult to explain why more officers did not take advantage of ambiguity and search in the weapons situation. Perhaps they had other alternatives in mind, such as calling for backup before searching. Future research should address this.

7. In contrast to the early days of the exclusionary rule, the public safety exception is now accepted by the Supreme Court and even in somewhat liberal state courts such as New York. The scenarios utilized in the survey did not go so far as to invoke these exceptions (see methodology section).

8. A case can be bright-line on one issue but ambiguous on certain points.

9. See Dixon (1997) for a discussion on the law with respect to police (although he emphasizes British policing).

CHAPTER 5

Extralegal Influences

To thoroughly explain police officers' decision-making processes regarding their legal authority, it is necessary to account for influences other than the law. There are countless outside factors that could have an impact on officers' legal behavior. Examining previous social science literature reveals that three factors are particularly relevant: the police culture, the community, and the police bureaucracy. Many of these social science studies, however, do not agree with each other about the level of impact—or, indeed, if there is an impact of these three factors on police legal behavior (see, e.g., Riksheim and Chermak, 1993). Anecdotal literature is even more perplexing. This chapter examines these outside influences and suggests the extent to which, if at all, these three extralegal factors influence officers' behavior with respect to the law.

THE POLICE CULTURE

The police culture emphasizes the importance of the group, particularly the influence of other officers (Crank, 1995; Drummond, 1976; Fielding, 1989; Manning, 1987; Reiss, 1971; Stoddard, 1968; Westley, 1970). It is sometimes called the informal code to distinguish it from formal rules. In general, this informal code stresses the need for officers to command respect from suspects, to band together, and not to trust the legal system.

Some have suggested that the negative impact of the police culture on officers is enormous. Indeed, euphemisms such as the "blue wall of silence" (police officers not cooperating with investigators or other competent authority regarding fellow officers who may be engaged in corruption or serious misconduct) or "testilying" (officers lying in court to ensure that evidence obtained illegally is admitted) certainly suggest that the police culture is able to defy organizational guidelines, community norms, and legal constraints and promotes wrongful behavior. There is a persuasive argument that such practices are widespread and endemic to the policing profession. Stoddard (1968: 227), for example, writes, "Illegal practices of police personnel are socially prescribed and patterned through the informal 'code' rather than being a function of individual aberration or personal inadequacies of the policeman himself."

Based on an abundance of scientific literature, we expect the police culture to have a destructive influence on officers; that is, it will tend to increase officers' illegal behavior (see, e.g., Brown, 1981; Black, 1970; Bayley, 1986; Lundman, 1994; Riksheim and Chermak, 1993; Sykes and Clark, 1975; Westley, 1970; Worden and Shepard, 1996). However, police departments continually deny that the police culture has such an impact. Former New York City Police Commissioner William Bratton (1996), for example, feels that police departments are in control of their officers. Another former New York City Police Commissioner, Howard Safir, also feels that such a culture is not the essence of officer behavior (see Cooper, 1997). Some recent research has also called into question the strength of the negative influence of the police culture, arguing in particular that one part of the police culture, the demeanor of a suspect (often called the attitude effect [explained earlier]), is not as strong an influence as legal factors (see especially Klinger, 1994). This is contrary to many other studies (see especially Worden and Shepard, 1996 and Lundman, 1994).

To determine the extent to which the police culture influences police officers' legal behavior, three specific aspects of the police culture were measured and assessed in the questionnaire administered to New York City officers: the distinctive language of police, the attitude (demeanor) of the suspect, and officers' loyalty to one another. Hypothetical situations were created based on the law as well as these three aspects of the culture. The situations were then manipulated in such a way that various legal and cultural situations were given to officers.[1] The researcher asked officers how they would respond to the given situation, assuming they were working the street. The legal situations included the car stop, person stop, weapon search, and drug search scenarios. The cultural situations involved using the language (without any other cultural aspects in the same situation), using a combination of the language and the attitude test, and utilizing a combination of the three aspects of the culture—language, attitude test, and loyalty.

To determine the influence of the language only, a short statement was included in which the suspect was described as a "skell." This word, familiar to NYPD officers, indicates someone who is acting in a nonconformist manner. This word was used without any other aspects in some situations to see how officers would react merely to the introduction of the distinctive language.

Another statement used to test the influence of the culture included both the language and the attitude test. This statement describes the suspect as "a mope who calls you an asshole." This statement uses both the language ("mope"—also basically someone acting in a nonconformist way) and the attitude test (the suspect's poor demeanor is indicated by calling the officer an "asshole"). Last, a cultural statement that invokes all three aspects of the culture was used. This is a statement describing the suspect as "a dirt-bag who, two months earlier, was arrested for attacking and severely injuring three fellow officers." This statement uses the language ("dirt-bag"), the attitude test (the suspect shows no respect by being a known cop fighter), and loyalty (the allegiance being tested is directed toward the officers who were previously injured).

Results

Results from the questionnaire indicate a much more complex influence of the police culture than one might expect on the basis of previous scientific literature. In one legal situation, merely adding the language had an influence; in another, only the situation that includes all three cultural aspects had an influence; and in the remaining two legal situations, the police culture did not have a significant influence on officers' conduct. To be more specific, all three aspects of the police culture (even mere words) had a significant impact on officers' judgments in the car stop situation, only a combination of all three aspects had an impact in the person stop situation, and no aspect of the police culture influenced officers in the drug or weapon situation.

Car Stop

In the car stop scenario the destructive influence of the police culture was particularly evident. With the mere introduction of the distinctive language (in this case the word "skell"), officers more than doubled their illegal behavior. For example, when the cooperative individual was to be stopped (i.e., no police culture influence was included), 14.8 percent of officers responded they would do the illegal stop (see Table 5.1). In contrast, when the car to be stopped contained a driver described as a "skell," the percentage of officers who stated they would illegally stop the car more than doubled to 32.5 percent. When a combination of police culture aspects was introduced into the car stop situation (where the car to be stopped contained a "mope" who called the officer an "asshole"), the number of officers doing the illegal stop again increased, to nearly 40 percent. Even though the majority of officers were working within legal guidelines, there is real cause for concern, in that the police culture obviously had a deleterious affect on officers' car stop behavior.

In the car stop situation, then, even the slightest aspect of the police culture (the language) had a significant affect on officers' stop behavior. The car stop situation is clearly illegal, and any increase in stop behavior needs to be closely scrutinized. In this case, even the slightest introduction of police culture tended to influence officers. *Apparently, officers are particularly sensitive to the police culture in car stop situations.*

Person Stop

In the person stop situation, which was highly ambiguous and probably illegal, the impact of the police culture was not as evident, though it did show some significant differences. Again, the majority of officers did not engage in the illegal behavior, regardless of the cultural impact.[2] However, there was a significant cultural impact on the situation in which all three aspects of the police culture were included. In the cultural situation that combines the distinctive language, the attitude effect, and loyalty (fellow officers were previously attacked), almost half (44 percent) of the officers responded that they would illegally stop the person. Comparing that response to the previous culture category (the "mope" who calls the officer an "asshole" [32.6 percent would stop the person]) shows a significant increase of 11.4 percent in stop behavior (44 percent − 32.6 percent).[3]

Accordingly, in the ambiguous person stop situation, something different occurred when all three aspects were present that caused officers to significantly increase their search behavior. The most important difference between this situation and the others was that this situation included an aspect which appeals to officers' loyalty to each other: the person the officer is dealing with is known to have severely injured three fellow officers.[4] Thus, when officers are stopping individuals, the police culture—in particular, a sense of loyalty to other officers—does adversely influence them.

Search Situations: Weapon and Drug

In both the weapon and drug search situations, there was no significant affect of the police culture on officers' legal behavior. For example,

Table 5.1
Illegal Bright-Line Car Stop Situation Cross Tabulation: Judgment By Police Culture*

	Police Culture				
Judgment	(1) Cooperative individual	(2) Skell	(3) Mope who calls you an asshole	(4) Dirt-bag who attacks fellow officers	Total
Not do the stop	247 (85.2%)	206 (67.5%)	205 (60.5%)	201 (63.2%)	859 (68.6%)
Do the stop	43 (14.8%)	99 (32.5%)	134 (39.5%)	117 (36.8%)	393 (31.4%)
Total	290 (100.0%)	305 (100.0%)	339 (100.0%)	318 (100.0%)	1,252 (100.0%)

*Gamma = .27, p < .0001.

in the weapon situation when it was illegal to search, 67.8 percent of officers stated they would not search when a cooperative individual was stopped (no aspect of the police culture was included). When all three aspects were included in the same illegal weapon situation, 67.4 percent of officers stated they would not search. Similarly, in the drug situation when it was illegal to search, 69.8 percent of officers stated they would not search when a cooperative individual was stopped (no aspect of the police culture invoked). When all three aspects were in the scenario for the same illegal drug situation, 72.4 percent of officers stated they would not search—a very slight increase in officers not searching (the opposite of what we expect).

The lack of influence of the police culture in the drug and weapon situations is important. This may be due to officers concentrating on other aspects, especially legal ones, when responding to these search situations. Perhaps the greater attention that courts, other agencies, and the police themselves have given to drug and weapon situations is having an impact on officers' field behavior. Also, since the culture did not have weight in search scenarios but it did have an influence in stop scenarios, there may be something different about the situations themselves that explains officers' varied responses. Perhaps the pressure of the culture is more important when explaining stop situations (e.g., car stops, person stops, arrests) than in other types of situations (e.g., searching, public encounters that may involve report writing or giving directions). It could be that arrest/stop situations are essentially focused on getting the person or car under immediate control (the focus is on officer authority and obtaining respect), whereas the other situations, including the dangerous gun situation, are focused on obtaining inanimate objects that are not as much of a threat to an *officer's personal authority* (regardless of the danger).

Overall, then, officers are not significantly biased by the police culture in search situations. Nevertheless, the police culture does seem to adversely influence officers in the car and person stop situations.

Theoretical Implications

Previous research suggests that certain aspects of the police culture will have a strong influence on police behavior. In particular, the "attitude test" (i.e., the influence of demeanor) is hypothesized to influence officers' behavior (e.g., Brown, 1981; Lundman, 1994; Worden and Shepard, 1996). The current materials, however, show that this effect may be situation-specific when explaining officers' *legal behavior*. Its influence was most pronounced in the car stop and to some extent in the person stop, but *not* in the search situations. Previous research tends to study this issue using other methods (i.e., observations) and concentrates on the arrest/

no arrest decision (see, e.g., Klinger, 1994). Thus, using a very different approach (a scientifically designed questionnaire), we show that the police culture does significantly influence officers' legal behavior, but that influence is limited to specific situations (i.e., car stop and person stop situations influence officers, but weapon and drug situations do not).[5]

While the police culture did adversely sway officers in the stop situations, the majority of officers remained within legal parameters even when the police culture was very strong in search situations. The influence of the police culture, then, is much more complex than previous study would suggest. Indeed, as previously stated in this book, the stereotypical view of police officers as generally rejecting legal guidelines is certainly much less plausible given the findings presented here. Certainly, further research is indicated to test these findings further.

THE COMMUNITY

The community can be a very enigmatic concept. There are many aspects of a community that could potentially impact officers' legal behavior: the politics of a neighborhood, geographic terrain, racial/ethnic composition, and many others. The scientific literature, however, strongly suggests the influence of one particular aspect of communities with respect to police legal behavior—community wealth. Considerable previous study, both empirical and anecdotal, suggests that community wealth is a significant factor explaining officers' legal behavior (see, e.g., Brooks, 1993; Riksheim and Chermak, 1993; Skolnick, 1966; Galliher, 1971; Chevigny, 1969).[6] These works suggest that the nature of the relationship is such that poor neighborhoods tend to be targets for police abuse of authority (e.g., illegal searches and/or stops).

Some have suggested that the race/ethnicity of a community is a more critical factor than community wealth. In fact, there is a major controversy regarding the influence of race in this area, known as racial profiling. Racial profiling occurs when law enforcement personnel stop people primarily on the basis of race and not of legal factors. The law does recognize, however, that race can be a legal factor which contributes to the development of reasonable suspicion. For example, if an officer has a description of a white male in his twenties, wearing a blue jacket, who is committing robberies in a drug-ridden neighborhood, officers do not have to disregard the race of the suspect (or the sex or other criteria), but use it in conjunction with other criteria to develop the level of proof required to legally stop a suspect (reasonable suspicion). This can complicate matters for those trying to study this issue.

For example, the Attorney General of the State of New York, Eliot Spitzer (1999), argues a disproportionate amount of minority persons are being stopped in New York City, especially compared to their representation in the population. He intimates that the NYPD is therefore engaging in racial profiling. The NYPD, however, vehemently argues that the Attorney General's analysis is flawed. Basically the NYPD argues that comparing the number of stops against the general population is incorrect; if a comparison is to be made, it should be against the criminal population on the street, because those are the people whom police can legally stop. The NYPD then showed that the racial breakdown of those people stopped closely correlates to crime complaints (NYPD, 1999).

We will not directly examine the issue of race with respect to its influence on officers' legal behavior—although we will view it indirectly (because many poor areas are predominantly minority). A major reason for not directly measuring race has to do with the fact that officers are all too aware of the controversial nature of this issue. Sensitivity training, including culture and ethnic identity lessons, are common in many police departments, including the NYPD. Officers are rigorously trained to be culturally aware and to treat people of minority groups in the same way they treat Caucasians. This is apparent in all forms of training—from recruit training to advanced in-service training. This training leads to at least two problems for a researcher.

First, based on focus groups with officers, it would significantly reduce the number of officers willing to respond to the questionnaire. Second, race becomes an exceedingly difficult concept to measure effectively. In fact, during development of the questionnaire, focus groups with officers indicated that including race would lead to what social scientists call socially biased responses—that is, officers would answer as they think others would want them to answer, rather than giving accurate responses. Using community wealth was also difficult. However, officers in focus groups indicated that community wealth would be more likely to evoke truthful responses.

A pretest of the questionnaire with a small sample of fifty officers using the wealthy/poor aspect of the community indicated not only that officers were willing to fill out and return the questionnaire but also that these officers were likely to be truthful. This was tested by correlating officers' responses with supervisors' evaluations of these officers' search/stop behavior. This, to some extent, confirms what the focus groups suggested.

Another reason for studying community wealth is that previous empirical research on race had been mixed, at best. For example, Riksheim and Chermak (1993: 361) state, "The majority of findings in the 1980's indicated that complainant's race has no effect." Also, in summarizing the literature on the arrest/no arrest decision, Riksheim and Chermak (1993:

365) write, "Utilizing a variety of data sets and examining various offenses, most of these studies found that race had no effect on police arrest decisions."

Our focus, then, is on the impact of community wealth on police legal behavior. To ascertain the extent to which community wealth influences officers' legal decisions, the questionnaire administered to New York City police officers was an excellent tool.[7] The survey design allows the researcher to manipulate the situation officers are placed in. Some of the questions place officers in poor neighborhoods and others in wealthy neighborhoods. Then officers were asked to determine whether they would do a behavior (using the hypothetical legal situations explained earlier), such as search or stop a person. In this way, one can determine the extent to which community wealth influenced officers' legal decisions in each of the court cases.

Results

Results from the questionnaire administered to New York City police officers clearly indicate that officers were not significantly influenced by the wealth of the community in any of the legal situations. In all four of the legal situations, community wealth did not have a significant impact on police officers' decisions (see Table 5.2). Indeed, comparing the average responses for each court case at each level of legality indicates that the responses are essentially indistinguishable from each other, regardless of the community wealth category. In the weapon situation, for example, when it was legal to search, the average of the responses in the wealthy neighborhood was 4.20; the average of the responses in the poor neighborhood was a comparable 4.27—an inappreciable difference. All the other situations similarly indicate very minor differences in the average responses. Additionally, neither the legal situation (weapon, drug, person stop, or car stop) nor the level of legality (legal, slightly ambiguous, highly ambiguous, illegal) affected the nature of this null finding.

Importantly, this agrees with research which suggests that neighborhood wealth has little to do with police intervention. For example, Fyfe et al. (1997: 466) write, "The nonsignificant area-poverty coefficient speaks against assertions that the social class composition of areas where police encounter citizens affects their decisions, at least in Chester, Pennsylvania." Similarly, Mastrofski et al. (1995) point out in their study based on ride-alongs in Richmond, Virginia, that *legal variables* such as evidence strength, offense seriousness, and the victim's preference show positive effects on the probability of arrest; extralegal variables such as race, gender, *wealth*, and personal reputation have inconsistent findings.

Table 5.2
Average Response to Survey—Community*

Level of Legality	Community**		Number of responses in category***
	Wealthy	Poor	
Weapon scenario			
Legal	4.20	4.27	963
Slightly ambiguous	4.11	4.19	932
Highly ambiguous	4.04	4.12	938
Illegal	3.39	3.17	923
Drug scenario			
Legal	5.69	5.56	924
Slightly ambiguous	5.99	5.97	940
Highly ambiguous	4.93	4.91	976
Illegal	3.28	3.01	910
Car stop scenario (bright-line) compared to	3.79	3.65	1,259
Person stop scenario (ambiguous)	3.37	3.27	1,252

*Based on average responses on a scale of 1 (not do behavior) through 8 (do behavior).

**Statistical tests show that there are no statistically significant differences between responses in poor neighborhoods versus wealthy neighborhoods.

***Respondents received 3 drug, 3 weapon, and 2 bright-line/ambiguous scenarios. Data are pooled, so a respondent can be responsible for answering more than one question within a category.

While the average of the responses by officers is essentially the same (comparing the responses across neighborhood wealth), there was another interesting finding that has theoretical implications. Some of the larger average differences (although they were still indistinguishable) were in the illegal situations. The largest difference in average judgments by officers, comparing the wealthy and poor neighborhoods, was in the category of illegal drug situations—a 0.27 difference. The next largest difference was in the illegal weapon situation, for which we see a 0.22 difference. The illegal car stop situation had a 0.10 difference. Interestingly, though the differences are essentially indistinguishable in each of these illegal situations, officers were *more likely to do the illegal act in the wealthy neighborhood*. These findings are particularly important because they have theoretical relevance.

Theoretical Implications

From a theoretical perspective, these findings on community wealth tend to refute the assertions of some criminologists. Certain criminologists, from the radical or conflict school, have suggested that police officers will tend to treat people in lower socioeconomic class neighborhoods with increased abuse of police power (see, for example, Reiman, 1990; Lynch and Groves, 1989; Vold and Bernard, 1986; Skolnick, 1966; Galliher, 1971). In general, this is based on radical theories which claim that officers, as agents of the ruling classes (i.e., the wealthy), will abuse their powers in poor areas in order to control the powerless. For example, Vold and Bernard (1986: 287) develop what they call a "unified conflict theory of crime."

In describing this theory, they suggest that "law enforcement agencies tend to process individuals with less, rather than more, political and economic power" (Vold and Bernard, 1986: 287). Also, in summarizing some of the studies on this topic, Brooks (1993: 150–155) writes, "Police have a tendency to be and act suspicious of residents in lower-class neighborhoods. [Also] . . . It is generally supported in the literature that individuals in the lower socioeconomic strata receive harsher treatment by the police."

While there may be other aspects of a community that influence officers, neighborhood wealth certainly did not impact upon New York City police officers' legal decisions. If anything, officers seem to be more illegal (regarding stops and searches) in *wealthy neighborhoods*—just the opposite of what some radical criminologists would predict (although, as we have seen, officers' legal behavior is basically indistinguishable across neighborhood types). It follows, then, that this survey refutes certain aspects of the conflict or radical point of view.

These data do, however, tend to support value statements made by police departments. Statements such as that officers will "impartially enforce the law" (NYCPD, 1997c: 3–6) are, at least to some extent, supported by the information collected here. Overall, based on the information collected from this study, police officers are not reacting differently, at least with respect to their legal behavior (i.e., searching and or stopping people), based on an area's poverty. Rather, legal criteria, such as developing reasonable suspicion, are far better at explaining officers' reactions.

POLICE BUREAUCRACY

Many researchers claim that the police agency itself is a major factor that influences officers to violate legal restrictions. Bittner (1974), for example, suggests that administrative regulation encourages bad police work. Reuss-Ianni (1983: 116–117) feels that "Street cops view bureaucratic controls as further confusing and compounding the difficulties they experience performing their job, rather than assisting them in dealing with the ambiguities and uncertainties." Brown (1981) believes that administrators are more inclined to tolerate abuses of the law compared to other officer misconduct.

Police administrators, however, see their organizations as highly successful in persuading officers to perform their duties legally. They suggest this is accomplished through management strategies, policies, and other means, regardless of what academics say (see especially Bratton, 1996). Formal written rules and regulations of police departments certainly indicate that police organizations are, at a minimum, attempting to follow the law and expect officers to do the same.

The specific wording of written agency policies, however, may not necessarily state the preferred behavior that the organization encourages. In fact, if illegal behavior is to be encouraged, this cannot be written for fear of lawsuits and/or other forms of retaliation. If some sort of illegal behavior is desired, say an illegal search and seizure, supervisors are more likely to hint (e.g., a wink and/or a nod) that they want such behavior rather than write a formal policy about conducting an illegal search. Other than written policy, management has at its disposal numerous tools to influence officer behavior, such as verbal statements to officers. For example, supervisors may state that they need more arrests and tolerate whatever conduct must be done to produce them.

The appearance given by police organizations, then, is that the agency wants supervisors to reinforce written rules and regulations. However, this is not necessarily the case. Rubinstein (1973: 401), for example, writes, "If they [supervisors] oblige their men to adhere to all of the legal rules, they will only reduce the number of vice arrests that are being made and cause their captains, divisional inspectors, and the chief inspector to demand increases . . . which will be accompanied with threats of transfer."

One well-known tool used by management in the New York City Police Department is the process called Compstat. Compstat attempts to control police behavior by focusing, to a great extent, on the power of higher-ranking officers, in particular the commanding officer (C.O.) of a precinct.[8] At Compstat meetings managerial personnel (higher ranking than the C.O.) hold the C.O. accountable for everything that occurs in the precinct, including especially, but not exclusively, crime statistics. Thus, pressures on C.O.'s at Compstat are varied but focus on reducing crime. This indirectly can mean putting pressure on officers to violate legal restrictions, such as search and seizure and stop and frisk, in order to make arrests and reduce crime. However, other pressures, such as organizational written policies, may pressure C.O.'s to follow legal constraints.

The Compstat process has received numerous accolades from police administrators and academicians alike (see Silverman, 1999). Its success has been considered tantamount to an upheaval in policing administration. Numerous police agencies are attempting to replicate the process in their jurisdictions (see especially Silverman, 1999).

In order to measure the impact of bureaucratic controls, we focused on the power of the C.O. To that end, five situations were created that test the impact of the police bureaucracy on police legal behavior. These situations are based on comments by a C.O. at a roll call (when officers receive their assignments before their shift begins). A critical aspect of these situations is the content of what the C.O. states to the officers.

In the first situation the C.O. states, "Inspections is in the precinct today." When a C.O. says this, he or she generally means that some form of formal authority outside the control of the C.O. is observing the activities of the officers in the precinct. This formal authority may include any number of outside units, such as the Quality Assurance Division, which generally checks precinct operations, including paperwork, whether officers are properly responding to radio calls, and other such matters. It could also mean the Borough Investigations Unit, which works under the direction of Patrol Borough for the precinct concerned, and investigates matters pertaining to misconduct of members of the police department.[9]

Additionally, patrol boroughs often assign a supervisor, usually with the rank of captain, to ensure that officers are properly performing their jobs. Formally, this person is called the Borough Patrol Supervisor—informally, he or she is called the "shoo-fly." The presence of any of these units or people represents one important type of authority that is responsible for ensuring the "proper behavior" of officers. "Proper behavior" in this case means behavior "outlined by guideposts, constitutions, job descriptions, history, and continual operational processes" (Fairfield, 1976: 14).

The second situation that measures the organization involves a statement by the C.O. referring to an inordinate number of civilian complaints being received. Civilian complaints result when someone who interacted with the police formally informs the Civilian Complaint Review Board (CCRB) that the officer used unnecessary force, abused authority (e.g., illegal stop/search), was discourteous, and/or used offensive language. Acquiring too many civilian complaints can be deleterious to an officer's career. Officers with many complaints (whether founded or unfounded) are often denied details (choice assignments) and have, in substantiated cases, been reprimanded with penalties that range from being warned and admonished to dismissal. The Patrolmen's Benevolent Association (PBA), the New York City police officers union, has claimed that the police organization in New York City unfairly discriminates against officers with many complaints. Additionally, they believe that the CCRB will negatively affect officer performance.

For example, in discussing how police officers will react to a civilian complaint review board (with no members of the police department on it), former PBA President Phil Caruso stated, "You're going to reach a point in time when the police are going to drop their hands and say, 'I'm not going to do anything out there.'" ("For Police," 1992: L25). McElroy and Goldstein (1992: A33) point out that "many officers believe their careers are hurt every time a complaint is lodged with the board. . . . Officers fearing that they could be hurt by even baseless complaints may avoid confrontational situations." Clearly, the impact of such formal bureaucratic influences as CCRB and Inspections needs to be explored to determine their influence on officers' legal behavior.

A third situation is a statement by the C.O., "Have a safe tour." This phrase is relatively innocuous. While this statement should have a minimal affect on officers' legal behavior and the first two statements by the C.O. should lower illegal behavior by officers, the fourth and fifth statements should cause officers to behave illegally. The fourth statement reads, "The precinct is down on felony arrests compared to last year's figures." This is an important statement not only because it tells officers that the commander is interested in more arrests but also because officers are keenly aware that the C.O. needs such arrests to defend him/herself at Compstat. Rubinstein (1973: 377), for example, touches on this issue. He writes about vice arrests, "If the patrolman were freed from having to make vice arrests, only the corrupt, the money hungry, would continue to do the illegal things so many policemen do."

Although the C.O. in the hypothetical scenario is not asking specifically for "vice" arrests, pressure is continually placed on officers to make arrests. For example, on "activity sheets," which are forms collected monthly by squad sergeants, officers must account for each and every arrest made. Favorable evaluations and choice assignments (e.g., anticrime [a coveted precinct-level plainclothes unit]) are often given based on the amount of activity an officer has.[10]

The fifth situation makes a personal appeal to officers and, importantly, adds a monetary incentive for officers to make an arrest—the availability of overtime. It reads, "Keep your sectors clean today; make arrests where possible. Overtime will be made available for all arrests. Don't be afraid to do your job. As long as your actions are not totally unreasonable, I personally will go to bat for you." Research supporting the use of money as a motivator includes a study by Drummond (1976). He feels that money is the main motivation for younger officers (aged twenty to thirty-five). Reuss-Ianni (1983: 85) also discusses this. She writes, "officers would deliberately make arrests at the end of the tour in order to make overtime money." Informally, this is known as "collars for dollars." Therefore, the inclusion of monetary incentives in the fifth statement is important to examining the affect of the organization on police legal behavior.

Thus, the police organization is measured using the comments of a C.O. at roll call. The content of those comments is important. The messages contain specific items supported by relevant literature aimed at measuring the affect of immediate (short-term) organizational influences on officers' legal behavior. These include the use of inspections, the influence of civilian complaints, the pressure to make arrests, and monetary incentives.

Results

Using the questionnaire administered to New York City officers indicated that the organization, as represented by the C.O.'s statements, had a very limited impact on officers' legal behavior. In essence, the results indicate that the police department neither increased officers' search/stop behavior through incentives nor decreased it with preventive measures. This is very evident in three of the four situations measuring the impact of the law—person stop, weapon search, and drug search. The impact of the police organization on officers' responses in these three situations was negligible.

The car stop situation, however, did contain one exception. In the car stop scenario, the fourth statement of the C.O. (in which the C.O. states that more arrests are needed) significantly increased the likelihood that officers would do the illegal stop. This finding is extremely sensible, since the car stop situation allows officers to be proactive in finding people to arrest and arresting them.

Proactive police work refers to those instances, much less frequent in policing, when a police officer initiates activity, such as a car stop. The vast majority of police work is thought to be reactive—basically doing what the public asks, such as responding to 911 radio calls. Certainly, initiating a car stop would give an officer a greater chance of making an arrest than would passively awaiting a radio call. However, the two other situations that would allow officers to be proactive in making an arrest, the person stop and the weapon search situation, did not show a similar increase in stop/search behavior. Again, the evidence indicates that car stops are an issue for police (also seen when examining the police culture).

The evidence collected here, then, shows that, except for the fourth statement in the car stop situation, the immediate or direct impact of the organization has little influence on precinct officers. In summarizing previous empirical literature on this topic, Riksheim and Chermak (1993) state that some studies have shown that supervision strategy has an insignificant or negative effect on officer-initiated encounters. That is, supervision may not be as critical a factor at explaining proactive police behavior. Two of the three proactive situations agree with Riksheim and Chermak's (1993) summary of previous work.[11] This includes the weapon search and the person stop situation. While the drug situation is reactive (the arrest is already made and the question posed to officers is whether they would search a container for drugs, not whether they would stop the person or search the person prior to arrest), it, too, showed no bureaucratic influence on officers.

The vast majority of statements by the C.O. had no influence on officers' legal behavior. One critical null finding is that when it comes to legal behavior, officers in general tend to ignore bureaucratic incentives such as money (i.e., availability of overtime). Authors conducting both qualitative and quantitative study on this issue have made various statements regarding how money can influence police behavior. For example, Bayley (1994: 67–68) writes, "police officers are preoccupied with monetary rewards." As stated, Drummond (1976) and Reuss-Ianni (1983) write about how officers are influenced by money. Mastrofski and Ritti (1993) also found that a small number of officers are responsible for numerous driving under the influence arrests due to monetary incentives.

While some officers may be heavily influenced by money, the current study shows that monetary rewards (i.e., availability of overtime) are not, in general, significant to explaining officers' decisions to search and/or stop. In fact, the fifth statement of the organization that included a monetary incentive did not have a strong influence in any of the situations. It may be, as some of the previous studies indicate, that only a very small group of officers are influenced by such rewards. This should be carefully examined by future research.

Interestingly, officers did not decrease their search/stop activity even when they were made aware that they were being observed by the Inspections Unit or that civilian complaints increased. Once again it seems that officers tend to ignore these agency controls. This is not to say that agency controls are meaningless. Indeed, the need for agency controls is seen in other variables such as the police culture. Rather, this research suggests that the influence of these controls is negligible with respect to *officers' legal behavior.* It may be that a few individual officers are influenced by these controls, but the vast majority do not consider them important factors in the calculus of determining their legal behavior.

Theory

Bureaucratic controls rarely influenced officers' decision-making with respect to the law. This means that the claims of many researchers that the bureaucracy of a police agency is a major factor causing officers to violate the law are certainly not supported by this research. Conversely, this also means that many of the management strategies aimed at controlling illegal behavior by officers was ineffectual. It is important to understand, however, that the role of the agency in influencing officers' legal behavior is not limited to the immediate rewards and punishments described here. Most significantly, it involves communicating the court rulings to officers and properly training them on how to act on them. This communication and training is a powerful force that has an enormous impact on officers, as demonstrated earlier. Baum (1985), for example, points out that properly transmitting the court rulings is one important factor in determining whether or not the court decision will be followed. Certainly, if officers are unaware of the law, there is no way that they can possibly be swayed by it. The training by the New York City Police Academy on the law is certainly to be commended. However, there were some issues in this data as well.

One issue has to do with the weakness of immediate rewards and punishments. The Compstat process suggests that the commanding officer is able to influence his or her officers to increase search/stop behavior at a whim. Further, this process would hold the C.O. accountable for the actions of the officers under his/her command. In this research, however, these higher ranking officers did not have as much influence as one might expect. Regardless of the content of their statements, most officers chose not to take the comments of the C.O. into consideration when searching and stopping suspects. Both possible rewards and punishments of the organization were dismissed by most officers as meaningless in their determinations of their legal behavior.

There was one notable exception to this general finding that needs to be explored further. In the proactive car stop situation, when the C.O. intimated that more arrests are needed, officers responded by conducting significantly more illegal stops. This leads to at least two important conclusions. First, similar to the finding in the police culture section, car stops seem to be a very troubling area for police with respect to their legal behavior.

Second, by grouping the responses to the fourth statement of the organization in the car stop situation by officer's assignment (the primary duty a particular officer tends to perform), we find that two groups of officers are particularly susceptible to the statements of the C.O. regarding arrests. The first susceptible group is anti-crime officers. These officers are in a very aggressive plainclothes crime-fighting unit and are expected to make some felony arrests each month. Importantly, they are appointed to that assignment by the precinct C.O. and therefore serve in that assignment at his or her discretion. Approximately 45 percent of these officers stated they would do the illegal car stop when the C.O. intimated that arrests were needed.

The second susceptible group includes those officers who have "inside the precinct assignments," such as crime prevention officers (assist the public in "target hardening"—making it more difficult to be a crime victim), community affairs officers (make liaison with members of the community), and domestic violence officers (review Domestic Incident Reports and try to reduce domestic violence). While it is to some extent expected that anti-crime officers would be proactive in conducting illegal car stops in order to make arrests, it is somewhat of a surprise to see inside officers also being proactive in this situation. In fact, more than half (60 percent) of these officers indicated that they would do the illegal stop. Importantly, these officers also are appointed to their assignments by the C.O. It may be that these inside officers have strong allegiances to the C.O., who keeps them in their choice inside assignments as opposed to answering radio calls.[12] This finding is one indication that only a very small number of officers are responsible for much of the work that the C.O. needs done as part of the Compstat process. It seems that a select few are responding to the needs of the organization.

Contrasting this finding with another paradigm for law enforcement—community policing—leads to some interesting conclusions. Community policing suggests that all officers should be involved in problem-solving efforts and that lower-ranking officers need to be empowered to do this. Compstat, on the other hand, generally directs change from the top down, using a centralized command structure and strictly holds the C.O. responsible for general crime in the precinct. This is an obstacle to properly developing a community policing model of policing:

> The focus of community policing is the development of collaborative police, community, and government partnerships to address problems and issues in neighborhoods. For these partnerships to develop, communities must first feel their input into self-governance is encouraged and is given serious consideration. . . . The reactive nature of their [police] work must change to a proactive approach. . . . All of this requires change in the traditional law enforcement structure. . . . Some law enforcement agencies appear open to community involvement for help in responding and adapting to change. Closed law enforcement agencies tend to strive for stability and are generally less responsive to their environment. They rely on centralized control through a bureaucratic management structure . . . officers cannot be held rigidly accountable for general crime in their area, they can be expected to try to address specific crimes and problems in the neighborhood. ("Leadership for the Transition to Community Policing," 2001: 51–52, 62)

It is possible that the NYPD, with appropriate progressive and insightful leadership, could benefit from adopting a more suitable community policing model.[13] This could motivate, empower, and enable many more officers (rather than the few who seem to be motivated by the organization now) to get involved in problem-solving efforts. Further, the officers so motivated in New York City were violating legal restrictions. By adopting a more suitable community policing model, officers may be able to solve problems and reduce crime without violating legal restrictions. Additionally, these community policing officers are more likely to take civilian complaints seriously, which would further reduce illegal activity (abuse of authority). As an example, work by Greene (1999) suggests that San Diego has achieved great success at reducing crime (similar to that in New York City) using a community policing model.

One example of how involving the community can be very effective in fighting crime is the use of the "AMBER Alert" system (America's Missing: Broadcast Emergency Response). Once police confirm a child has been abducted, descriptions of the child and the perpetrator, including automobile information, is broadcast through the Emergency Alert System (formerly the Emergency Broadcast System—the same is used for weather emergencies) on radio, television, and cable systems. Often this will include electronic signs on bridges and highways as well. By soliciting the help of the public, the police are much more likely to capture the suspect and save the child. This is merely one example that aptly demonstrates how a community policing model, in which communities and the police work as partners, is a powerful method to fight crime. Additionally, because police officers are working closely with community members, it is less likely that members of the community will complain. Using the AMBER alert example, innocent community members who are stopped because they resemble the description being broadcast are more likely to understand why they are being stopped and therefore will be less likely to file complaints against the police.

SUMMARY

Social science literature has identified three extralegal factors that are particularly important to explaining police behavior with respect to obeying court decisions: the police culture, the community, and the police bureaucracy. Using the questionnaire administered to New York City officers, this chapter closely examines these three extralegal factors. The police culture is an informal code that stresses the need for officers to maintain respect, to unite together, and not to trust the legal system. Results indicate that there was destructive influence of the culture in the person and car stop legal situations. In the car stop situation, the police culture was particularly influential—up to 40 percent of officers indicated they would conduct an illegal car stop. Community wealth had little or no influence on officers' legal behavior. This contradicts assertions by radical criminologists that police are more likely to abuse their authority in poor communities. The vast majority of statements testing the influence of the police bureaucracy also had very little effect on officers' legal behavior. One exception to this general finding was in the proactive car stop situation, in which officers significantly increased their illegal behavior. Interestingly, those who were most influenced in the car stop situation were officers who work in anti-crime units and officers who had administrative assignments. It is suggested that the NYPD might benefit from adopting a more suitable community policing model such that officers are more motivated by immediate department rewards and punishments.

NOTES

1. The factorial survey method used for this project allows manipulation of many other aspects of police behavior in the same scenario. For the purposes of

presentation, this book simplifies the more complicated models that were, and can be, accomplished using this method.

2. Since this situation is ambiguous, it is not definitely illegal.

3. One must be careful in this situation not to compare the car stop situation with the person stop situation. It would be an inappropriate comparison because one legal situation is bright-line and the other is legally ambiguous. That is, the fact that more officers are doing the illegal stop in the person stop situation is more likely due to ambiguity of the legal situation than to differences in the culture.

4. Note that the slightly larger mean difference between *level 4* and *level 3* does *not* show up in the multivariate analysis since, in the multivariate models, we are comparing the difference in means between level 1 and each of the other levels (multivariate mean difference between levels 4 and 1 is 0.515; bivariate difference in means between levels 4 and 3 is 0.60) (see the Appendix for an explanation of the levels).

5. One cautionary note on this issue: the survey also indicated that an officer's perception of community *respect* was significant in some of the scenarios. Although the community respect variable was weak, it is yet another indicator that demeanor (at the community level) significantly influences officer behavior. Thus, if anything, this study suggests that police culture variables (especially suspect/community demeanor) need to be more completely explored by future researchers (with methodological issues more fully addressed).

6. Regarding empirical study, especially with respect to the arrest/no arrest decision, see Riksheim and Chermak (1993: esp. 369).

7. At the end of the questionnaire officers were given an open-ended question asking for their input. Interestingly, a very small number of officers (19) objected to the inclusion of a question on the wealth of the neighborhood.

8. Others also go to these meetings, such as Housing Police Service Area C.O.'s and Transit District C.O.'s, as well as supervising detectives.

9. The formal name of this unit sometimes changes with different administrations. However, precinct personnel generally use the Inspections title.

10. Reuss-Ianni (1983) also discusses this issue.

11. In the drug situation, an arrest has already been made, and therefore there is less opportunity for officers to be proactive.

12. However, this finding should be read carefully, since categorizing the officers into anti-crime and inside officers and examining only the car stop situation reduces the number of responses in each assignment category to ten and eleven, respectively.

13. The NYPD did attempt to adopt a community policing model in the 1980s and 1990s, with dismal results (e.g., officers taking weekends off, crime rampant). Further, NYPD still claims to be doing community policing. I am suggesting that the NYPD should alter whatever community policing they may be doing such that it is more effective and appropriate to their needs.

CHAPTER 6

Learning from the New York City Experience

The New York City experience in aggressive crime-fighting is well suited to developing a comprehensive understanding of how police officers behave in an intense crime control environment with respect to the law. We have seen that officers generally obey legal guidelines. In almost every situation more than half of officers were working within legal parameters. However, there were some very important areas of concern. First, when laws are written unclearly, officers are influenced by that ambiguity. Slight ambiguity in laws is used by officers to their advantage, meaning more officers will search and/or stop in mildly ambiguous legal situations. When the law is extremely ambiguous, especially in dangerous situations, it appears that officers will stretch the law to its very limits, taking advantage of every bit of ambiguity left to them.

Additional concerns were exposed when examining the three primary extralegal factors: the police culture, the community, and the police bureaucracy. In stop situations, particularly car stops, the deleterious influence of the police culture was particularly evident with up to 40 percent of officers electing to carry out an illegal stop. Community wealth and the immediate sanctions of the police bureaucracy had little influence on police officers' legal behavior with one important exception. Certain officers were more likely to conduct illegal car stops when their commanding officer suggested that more arrests were necessary. Officers assigned to anti-crime and administrative duties were particularly susceptible to the commanding officer's suggestion.

These results are consistent with my experience as a police officer in New York City. For example, I can recall times where arrests were needed and proactive car stops were conducted for disobeying traffic regulations, particularly in areas that were known for illegal activity. Also, officers were much more likely to conduct a search when they suspected a weapon was in the car. At times, the law was stretched to its limit. Nevertheless, most of the time officers worked within legal guidelines. Using these experiences and combining them with empirical results from the questionnaire help us to better understand the dynamics of how the law influences police behavior. In this chapter, the results from previous chapters are discussed with a particular emphasis on practical lessons that can be extracted from these results.

THE POLICE CULTURE

Regarding the police culture, a sense of loyalty to other officers was seen as important to explaining police legal behavior in both person and car stop situations. Many researchers have discussed the problem of group loyalty and policing. For example, Alderson (1979: 67) writes, "The required loyalty to the group as a necessary adjunct of superior policing is corrupted into an alien form. It becomes loyalty to the group above the police as a whole and even above the law itself. This kind of group solidarity spells disaster." Armed with the knowledge that this sense of loyalty has a significant impact on officers in both car and person stops, police administrators, the courts, and researchers should carefully monitor car and person stop situations especially when the law is unclear.

Person Stop Situations

Police departments must consider collecting data on every person stop situation. The NYPD has been, and continues to be, at the forefront of data collection with respect to person stops. In March 1999, the NYPD commenced creating a computerized database containing all recorded person stops since 1994. At the time Police Department policy did not require officers to record all stops, but only certain stops that fit a list of criteria, such as when the suspect was stopped by force or when the suspect was frisked. However, since January 1, 2001, all officers have been required to record every stop situation based on reasonable suspicion that the suspect has committed, is committing, or is about to commit a crime (i.e., all *Terry v. Ohio*–type stops).[1]

The information on person stops is recorded using a Stop, Question, and Frisk Report. A revised Stop, Question, and Frisk Report came into use on January 1, 2001. This relatively new form makes use of check-off boxes that simplifies the recording of information and allows sophisticated data analyses. It provides a vast array of information about stops, including the amount of force used, the legal justification for the stop/frisk/

search that took place, pedigree (e.g., name, date of birth, age, height, weight, sex, race, etc.), and other basic information, such as the location of the stop. This new form has generally received favorable comments, even from the New York Civil Liberties Union (see Marzulli, 2001: 2).

Until recently members of the NYPD were required only by department policy to fill out these forms. However, since 2002 it is required by a local law under Section 14-150 of the New York City Administrative Code (called the "Vallone Bill") to report statistics based on these reports to the City Council. This form, then, is an excellent tool for checking and balancing police power with respect to stops. Not only can the NYPD more effectively monitor stops internally, but it can also provide data quickly to oversight bodies such as the City Council.

Car Stops

As has been demonstrated, the police culture has a very detrimental influence on officers in car stop situations. Indeed, car stops are one of the most controversial areas for police. Previous study has indicated that evidence from car stop situations is often suppressed in court (see especially Spiotto, 1973). Furthermore, police car pursuits often end in situations that involve brutality (see especially Worden, 1992).

While many agree that car stops are a concern, numerous departments overlook recording basic information about them. The NYPD is no exception. Unlike person stops, police officers in the NYPD do not record information about ordinary car stops.[2] The typical practice in the United States is to record neither person stops nor car stops. However, given the damaging influence of the police culture on these types of incidents, accurately recording information about *every* car stop (as the NYPD does in person stop situations) would seem appropriate.

In 2000, the United States Department of Justice released *A Resource Guide on Racial Profiling Data Collection Systems,* by Deborah Ramirez, Jack McDevitt, and Amy Farrell. This guide makes specific recommendations for traffic-stop data collection systems. Some of the data that they suggest police agencies routinely collect for all vehicle stops include date, time, and location of stops; license number, state, and description of vehicle stopped; length of stop; name and identification number of the officers who initiated or participated in the stop; date of birth, gender, race/ethnicity of the stopped individual; the reason for the stop; and whether a search was conducted.

Providing information about both person and car stops will help to identify those officers who are abusing their authority. This can be accomplished in a number of ways. One method for supervisors to identify abusive officers is to review the paperwork on the stops for patterns of abuse. For example, supervisors could look for officers who conduct what appear to be legally questionable stops. Those officers who do not have a sufficient legal basis for a car stop need to be identified and retrained or disciplined. However, this task is more difficult than one might assume. The United States Supreme Court in the case of *Whren v. United States* (1996) allows police officers to stop a car based on probable cause that any violation occurred.[3] Officers can claim, for example, they were making a car stop for, say, a broken headlamp, when, in fact, they were stopping the car because they had a hunch—merely suspected—it was transporting drugs. The probable cause the officer has for the violation of the broken headlamp justifies the stop regardless of the ulterior motive of the officer. Given this legal power, supervisors will have to be very innovative in developing strategies to determine those officers who are abusing their authority.

Departments that are technologically capable can create a data set from the information collected as previously suggested and analyze it using powerful statistical tests. These tests allow management and supervisors to determine how officers are performing in a more sophisticated manner than simply reviewing paperwork. Using proper statistical analyses, one can more easily identify patterns that a nonsophisticated eye might miss. For example, officers who are stopping well above the average number of minority motorists can easily be identified, and possibly questioned and/or investigated regarding this activity. Other analyses, such as tests of statistical significance, would also be helpful.

Importantly, other computer software packages allow this information (if it is properly captured) to be mapped. This can be very valuable in determining patterns by providing a clear visual image of where stops are occurring. Also, when combined with arrest data and complaint data, these maps would allow supervisors to determine whether car stops are being conducted in areas where they would be most effective at reducing crime. For example, if there are many car thefts in a certain neighborhood, officers should be conducting car stops in or near that area. In the NYPD, mapping has been an integral part of the Compstat process in fighting crime. Mapping as I propose it would complement crime-fighting by helping to identify officers who are abusing their authority.

There are many other prudent measures that police departments can take to combat the deleterious effects of the police culture. One important tactic is to increase supervision of officers at car stops. Frontline supervision should carefully monitor communications for car stops. Supervision should proactively seek to observe officers while they are doing car stops. During these observations supervisors need to note officers who are properly conducting stops and those who are not. Using appropriate management techniques, supervisors need to correct officers who are conducting questionable stops (e.g., one general rule is punish in private, praise in public). Supervisors could also make themselves visible to officers at car stops, thus helping to keep officers on their best behavior. Not only does this increase in supervision help to alleviate the negative aspects of the culture, it also keeps officers safer, since supervisors will be nearby for backup as necessary. Of course, this assumes that supervisors are properly trained and performing their duties correctly.

Increased training that desensitizes these destructive cultural influences would also be helpful. To be most effective, training programs on car stops must emphasize not only the danger of the situation (typical at many police academies) but also the adverse impact of the police culture. In particular, officers should be made aware of the detrimental influence of (1) the demeanor of the suspect, (2) the way other officers describe a person (e.g., mope), and (3) the influence of loyalty to other officers. Officers must be rigorously trained to consider legal criteria (e.g., constitutional rights) and not these extralegal factors. Further, this training must constantly be reinforced. Lessons in the classroom must accurately reflect a total commitment by management. Field supervisors need to send the same messages as classroom instructors.

One way to encourage this would be to include a measure of behavior at car stops in both supervisor and officer evaluations. However, a total commitment requires a paradigm shift (a change in the basic philosophy of the organization), such as the shift to community policing, but that may be very difficult for some agencies. As stated earlier in this book, if an agency adopts an appropriate community policing model, then these and other suggested changes would more likely take place and remain in place.

One of the more technologically advanced methods to assist with supervision at car stops is the use of audio and video equipment installed in police vehicles and aimed at suspect vehicles. These are especially helpful for viewing individual situations or officers. However, even though individual incidents are captured on this equipment, it is much too time-consuming for supervisors to view the vast number of car stops that take place, which limits its effectiveness as a supervisory tool. Also, the use of such equipment is very expensive and is limited to a very short span of coverage. For example, once the suspect or officer is out of range of the camera or microphone, it will no longer be effective. Nevertheless, for agencies that can afford this equipment, it is certainly another method of oversight.

BRIGHT-LINE SITUATIONS

Properly alleviating the damaging influence of the police culture, especially in car and person stop situations, is one important lesson that can be gleaned from the evidence previously outlined. Another lesson is based on what we saw when we compared officers' responses to a bright-line illegal situation versus their responses to a situation based on a convoluted court decision. Officers responded by doing illegal behavior less often when the court explicated a rule in clear terms. That is, in the bright-line case officers tend to do the illegal car stop significantly less often compared to the ambiguous person stop case.

Evidence of the difficulty with ambiguity in the law is also seen in the questionnaire where officers' responses varied widely according to the situation. In the drug situation, when the scenario was very ambiguous (nearly illegal), officers decreased their search activity. However, in the weapon situation, when officers were placed in a similar ambiguous situation, they increased their search activity. This indicates that ambiguity in the law not only makes it difficult to circumscribe officer behavior but also that officers' behavior will be less predictable, and possibly more vulnerable to legal challenge. Again, this suggests that bright-line rules will help reduce questionable behavior on the part of officers.

Based on these findings, it seems reasonable to suggest that, where possible, bright-line rules should be incorporated into court decisions, laws, and department policies that aim to circumscribe officers' authority. That is, to help prevent officers from straying beyond the boundaries of the law, clear and concise rulings seem to help. Many distinguished scholars have crusaded for more clarity in the law, among them Baum (1985), Grano, (1982), LaFave, (1974), and Whitebread, (1985).

The United States Supreme Court has, at times, explicated the need for bright-line rules.[4] In fact Linda Greenhouse, a 2002 Pulitzer Prize–winning *New York Times* Supreme Court reporter, gave a lecture in March 2002 suggesting that one of the main dividing lines for the Court is on the issue of bright-line rules. She suggested that some justices on the Court, led by Justice Antonin Scalia, favor giving direction to lower courts and practitioners, while others, led by Justice Stephen Breyer, feel that cases should be decided on a fact-specific basis. She calls this maximalism (bright-lines) versus minimalism (fact-specific).[5]

While it might appear from Greenhouse's lecture that this is also a conservative versus liberal argument—Scalia's maximalist position being conservative and Breyer's minimalist position being liberal—the bright-line debate unquestionably crosses these standard ideological lines. We see this in specific examples of cases in which bright lines have been suggested by the Supreme Court, such as *California v. Acevedo* (1991), *Dunaway v. New York* (1979), and *New York v. Belton* (1981). Importantly, the *Dunaway* decision is an example of a case favoring bright-line rules written by one of the Court's most liberal members in its history, Justice William Brennan.

However, the case for bright-line rules is not as simple as one might assume. In fact, some argue vehemently against them (e.g., Alschuler, 1984; Heffernan and Lovely, 1991; Howard, 1994; Rothwax, 1996). Alschuler (1984: 227) sums up this position thus, "Rules tend to limit the importance of subjective judgment, to promote equality, to control corruption, to simplify administration, and to provide a basis for planning before and after controversies arise." He goes on to critique the rules argument by saying, "When the best rules that our powers can devise produce injustice often enough, we do well to abandon them even at the price of lawlessness." He then argues for a rule of "reasonableness."

At a minimum his argument points out how difficult an issue this can be. However, without a clear rule for police, how are the police supposed to react? He might say as a "reasonable cop" should. Unfortunately, this leads to numerous interpretations. One court will allow an act while another will not. Such flexible rules often lead to politically expedient solutions. Bright-line rules can be difficult to construct, especially for courts, which can hear a case only when it is brought before it. Nevertheless, unless the courts wish to relinquish authority to police, these rules are necessary.

Legislatures and police agencies, through policy statements, also need to compose in bright-lines. Even Alschuler's argument against bright-line rules contains important reasons to have them: limiting subjectivity, promoting equality, controlling corruption, simplifying administration, and providing a basis for planning. Indeed, these are strong arguments for bright-line rules. His main objection is that the rules lead to "injustice." However, if a rule is that bad, then change the rule—do not abandon using rules altogether. There are too many important reasons to use them prudently.

There are also practical problems in policing that point to the need for bright-line rules. At times, officers cannot do a balancing act in the streets, carefully weighing the rights of all sides. There is often no time for a reasoned debate of the issues. Furthermore, what is "reasonable" in one jurisdiction may not be reasonable in another. The need for officers to make quick decisions and the need to establish minimum standards are two reasons for legislating bright-line rules. It seems that legislatures, courts, and police agencies which are ambiguous in their direction are merely abdicating their responsibility.

For example, before the Supreme Court case of *Tennessee v. Garner* (1985), it was permissible in some jurisdictions to shoot an unarmed, fleeing felon. The officer in *Garner* did precisely that. Perhaps, at the moment, the officer's actions seemed reasonable to him. However, upon reflection we can see how a simple rule could easily have prevented this horrible loss of life. As Justice Byron White wrote in *Garner*, "a police officer may not seize an unarmed, non-dangerous, suspect by shooting him dead." At the time of the *Garner* decision, the New York City Police Department had specific guidelines addressing this type of situation. Unfortunately, the department in Tennessee did not. The officer had far *too much discretion*. In that split second, the officer took a life that could have been saved had a simple rule been in effect. The officer in this case, and undoubtedly officers in many others, made what the Court, and hence society, feels is an incorrect judgment. It is very likely that many officers think they are being reasonable at the time of their actions, but later, upon reflection, realize their actions were questionable. Guidelines are needed to prevent such occurrences from happening. Hence, the rule *do not shoot an unarmed, non-dangerous, fleeing felon*. This offers much more guidance as to society's expectations. The officer in the field, no matter how professional, cannot be expected to make split-second decisions based on ambiguous rules. *This is unfair to the officer, to the suspect, and to society.* Where possible, we owe it to all to attempt to give guidance. It is the same with searches, seizures, and stops; the courts, legislators, and policymakers need to go on the record, to guide frontline practitioners.

Will a guideline, such as the one drafted in the *Garner* decision, actually influence police behavior? The current study indicates that it will. Other research has indicated this as well. For example, Tennenbaum (1994) points out that the impact of the *Garner* decision was powerful, especially in jurisdictions that allowed shooting of fleeing felons. Further, since many departments, including New York City, had restrictive, yet workable, guidelines in place well before *Garner*, this suggests that the expertise of police departments needs to be more fully explored by courts so that they can write laws which are not only reasonable but also workable and based on practical experience. Thus, the evidence of this study suggests (even in comparatively innocuous search and seizure and stop and frisk laws) that officers tend to follow clear guidelines. Clear, concise rules to the extent possible are necessary.

Nevertheless, there are situations where they may be unwarranted, where problems occur with rules. However, clear rules are the best possible way to protect our rights and give guidance to those who enforce the law. If a rule does not work properly, it should be rewritten with the insights and wisdom gained from the incident(s) that brought about any wrongdoing. In this way, officers learn from the past, with rules being changed as errors are made.

Contrast this with a fact-specific method of lawmaking (policymaking), in which no rules are made and little or no guidance is provided by past errors because the facts of every situation differ. Mistakes will be made over and over again. While this method does have advantages, such as allowing great discretion for the enormous variety of situations, if a rule can be written that will capture the vast majority of situations, it should be composed such that frontline practitioners are given some guidance. When lawmakers and policymakers fail to write a rule where they can, *they are shifting responsibility* to the frontline practitioner by failing to explain what is expected. Certainly lawmakers and policymakers share some responsibility for the *Garner* shooting with the officer due to their failure to guide the officer properly before the tragic incident occurred. How many other tragedies could have been avoided?

The need for intelligible rules is especially important to police officers who are implementing these decisions on the street. A lack of guidance from the courts, legislatures, and policymakers leaves police officers in a very precarious position. Officers, although they have some training in legal restrictions, are not lawyers or judges. Yet even lawyers and judges under calm conditions have enormous difficulty with the guidelines of the law of the Fourth Amendment or its counterpart in state constitutions. How do the courts, legislatures, and indeed the American people expect officers with limited expertise, and under less than ideal conditions (sometimes under enormous stress, with only seconds to make a decision), to properly execute incomprehensible rulings?

Some could argue that, especially in dangerous situations (e.g., shootings, searching for weapons), we should leave the law ambiguous. However, my research indicates that such ambiguity will lead some officers to abuse their authority. Also, such ambiguity in the law could place officers' and others' lives in jeopardy through situations such as *Garner*. Last, lives could be jeopardized in another way. There was a group of officers, for example, who were *not* searching in the weapon scenarios even when it was legal to do so. In fact, approximately 71 percent of officers in the weapon situation were unsure or definitely not searching when it was legal to do so. These officers may be so vexed by numerous and conflicting legal restrictions that they respond by not doing any searches. At times not searching, while legally safe, can be dangerous to field officers and the people they are sworn to protect.

THE COMPSTAT PROCESS

Other lessons can be learned by closely scrutinizing the practices of the NYPD with respect to aggressive crime-fighting. Many jurisdictions are in the process of replicating the New York City Police Department's Compstat process. These jurisdictions in particular should consider the implications of these findings in order to fully and more properly adopt a Compstat program. This work shows both positive and negative aspects of the Compstat process. The good news is that officers in New York City are generally following legal guidelines, even under the pressures to fight crime. However, there are some very troubling aspects of this program, especially when it was first launched in New York City.

One major concern with the Compstat model is the extreme emphasis (perhaps overemphasis) on crime-fighting rather than on other, equally important, aspects of policing: protecting the constitutional rights of citizens, officers working within legal boundaries (e.g., without illegal search and seizure and/or stop and frisk violations), morale of police officers and supervisors, and community discontentment with police. It is not implied that the NYPD does not attempt to address these issues; rather, the extreme emphasis on crime-fighting and crime reduction has effectively made these other important issues less critical. This was especially true in the first several years in which Compstat was operating, and is now the model utilized by many other organizations. Consequently, while crime has been reduced to record levels (certainly a major accomplishment—assuming the NYPD was responsible for the reduction), there are other issues that have become less imperative and require further attention by agencies and researchers. We now turn to developing a deeper, theoretical understanding of these concerns as they relate to the Compstat process.

Style of Policing

In 1994, when Compstat began, there was a radical alteration in the style of policing in the NYPD. This radical alteration may not have been appropriate to every community in New York City—which is extremely diverse. To understand this, an overview of some basic work on styles of policing is necessary.

James Q. Wilson, in his classic work, *Varieties of Police Behavior* (1977), studied eight communities and argued that one of three basic styles of policing was prevalent in each. These are not absolute styles; rather, one style becomes more prevalent compared to the others. These styles are called service, legalistic, and watchman. The essence of these styles can be defined as follows: legalistic—police make many arrests/summonses, as if there is one community standard; watchman—the main concern of police is with maintaining order; service—police take all requests seriously but are less likely to respond with a formal sanction (e.g., arrest, summons). Wilson (1977: 143) argues that the most prevalent style will depend on many factors, such as socioeconomic composition of the community, the law enforcement standards set, the political system, and the concerns of the police chief. The municipality or community being policed is extremely important. For example, regarding the service style, Wilson (1977: 200) writes, "This style is often found in homogeneous, middle-class communities in which there is a high level of apparent agreement among citizens on the need for and definition of public order but in which there is not administrative demand for a legalistic style." Using Wilson's styles, we can better understand the New York City experience with policing.

In the New York City Police Department a community policing/ problem-solving approach was adopted in the 1980s and early 1990s. Generally, this approach is similar to Wilson's service style. Officers were sent out in large numbers, taking all calls seriously and working closely with communities while tending not to use formal sanctions. This meant *not* making arrests unless appropriate, and basically being visible—a friendly beat cop approach.[6] This style was more service-oriented and empowered individual officers to make key decisions.

The Compstat process *drastically* changed this. Commanding officers under Compstat are held strictly accountable for the crime that occurs in their precincts. This focus on crime reduction has brought a highly bureaucratic, authoritative, top-down management style to the NYPD. Evidence of this is seen at Compstat meetings, where the entire executive staff as well as visitors (often executives from other departments throughout the world) observe a commander as he or she addresses precinct crime problems. Rather than acting like the friendly beat cop, high-level department executives quite often publicly berate commanding officers of precincts for failure to reduce crime.

The result of this emphasis on "crime and commanding officers," as opposed to "service and the beat cop," is that the NYPD developed a more legalistic style as opposed to a service-oriented approach. Since the driving engine for Compstat is crime statistics, there is pressure on all ranks to reduce the number of crime reports and increase the enforcement statistics (e.g., summonses and arrests). Under this approach, police officers have little or no control over their behavior; arrest, summons, or other formal sanctions become mandatory so that they can be reflected in the precinct Compstat statistics.

Other than possibly reducing crime, this legalistic approach has vast consequences. One consequence is based on New York City's being a very diverse community. Because it is so diverse, a consensus about how police should behave has *not* emerged. Under the community policing approach, local communities had input into how they would be policed. There was an attempt to involve diverse communities by meeting their identified needs. The key was to work with each community to determine and root out problems that cause crime. Police were partners with communities.

Under the legalistic style adopted, all communities are treated similarly, as if one community standard exists—an implied consensus about the law and its enforcement. Since there is a lack of agreement, some communities will inevitably be very dissatisfied with police behavior. In particular, minority communities have been outspoken about their discontent (see, e.g., Haberman, 1997).[7] For example, minority communities have been particularly critical of the NYPD regarding incidents such as the sexual abuse of Abner Louima and the shootings of Amadou Diallo and Patrick Dorismond, as well as alleged racial profiling. It is often asserted that these events are due to the style of policing in New York City.

To review, in 1994 the NYPD rapidly adopted a legalistic style of policing, as opposed to the service style of previous years, when implementing the Compstat process in the name of reducing crime.[8] This has apparently had both positive and negative effects. On the negative side, for example, it has led to alienation of many communities—especially those which disagree with the dominant culture group. On the positive side, crime has decreased drastically. A closer examination of two key areas of Compstat, leadership and the influence of aggressive policing on officer behavior, helps us to further understand the ramifications of this process.

Leadership

In general, many police leaders mistakenly adopt top-down leadership styles in the belief that they are embracing a military model of leadership (Cowper, 2000). Such a style of leadership has consequences. As Cowper (2000: 237) states:

> This style of leadership (not even a true representation of leadership by boot camp drill instructors) has done within policing exactly what its critics decry: created organizations that are centrally controlled and highly inflexible, characterized by top-down order transmission and bottom-up reporting; less creative and more intellectually rigid individual officers bound to tradition and regulations, unable to deal effectively with both the dynamics of modern policing theories and the communities they serve; and a more

combat/enforcement-oriented force, with a resulting increase in isolation from and hostility between police and citizens.

Although the NYPD is making vast strides to change the Compstat process, as I will discuss, the process as it was initially formed was based on a military model. In fact, former Chief of Department Louis Anemone, a main player in the Compstat process, was often referred to as "General Patton."[9] As Cowper (2000: 242) writes, "Compstat is a highly simplified form of military operational planning that uses tactical and strategic intelligence data to drive operations . . . [yet] it fails to seek and understand the theories and concepts behind the method." Essentially Compstat was rule by fear.[10] Commanding officers at Compstat feared presenting, since top brass would badger and berate them in public. Descriptions such as a "war on crime in New York City" furthered the imagery of the military.

The top-down leadership style of Compstat also alienated those on the lower end, Captains and below. For example, Flynn (2000: A1) writes about a recently retired captain with thirty years of service:

> Captain Costello's primary complaint was not pay, but what he viewed as the numbingly relentless demand to top his own arrest or summons numbers. "Nothing was good enough.". . . In 1997, for example, . . . his officers were fortunate enough to stumble onto a large crowd of teenagers drinking in a plaza along Fifth Avenue and issued hundreds of summonses. The following year, though, the teenagers were not there. Still . . . he feared he would be chastised if his summons numbers dropped. So his plainclothes officers found themselves skulking in doorways. . . . "You are so desperate to get these summonses . . . ," Captain Costello said.

Some basic concepts of bureaucracy help to elaborate on this issue. One of the key differences between pre- and post-Compstat NYPD is the type of bureaucracy. At NYPD there is an attempt to maximize work efficiency by reducing crime numbers without any emphasis on the role of the people within the organization. The sociologist Max Weber listed the basic characteristics of the typical bureaucracy (i.e., a scientific management approach) and their positive and negative aspects: division of labor, hierarchy of authority, written rules and regulations, and impersonality (Schaefer, 2001: 151). The positive aspects include efficiency, clarification of who is in command, workers being aware of expectations, and reduction of bias. Applicable negative aspects include depriving employees of a voice in decision-making, goal displacement, concealment of mistakes, discouraging loyalty to the organization, and feelings of alienation (Schaeffer, 2001: 152).

A very different management approach is called the human relations approach. This approach considers the role of individuals within the organization: their feelings, frustrations, and needs. Compstat could benefit from utilizing principles of this approach. For example, the commander who is considered part of a team rather than publicly berated for failure to reduce crime is more likely to be content in his/her work environment. Contrast this with the commander who is publicly berated—more likely than not, he or she will influence his/her subordinates negatively (e.g., Captain Costello). Additionally, a berated commander will likely feel alienated and may try to resolve the issue by developing informal rules (e.g., promoting illegal stops).

Indeed, crime statistics themselves may be subject to manipulation as a result of this scientific management approach. This is due to overwhelming pressures to reduce crime. Commanders will become very innovative in developing techniques to ensure that, at a minimum, there appears to be a reduction in crime. For example, one can give the appearance of a crime reduction by counting only those incidents that precisely fit the explicit legal definition of a particular crime. This technique can best be understood by studying the constructionist viewpoint of deviance.

Constructionists essentially argue that deviance, in this case crime, is a manifestation of how that crime is defined. Regarding the NYPD, prior to Compstat, few, if any, judgments were made about the accuracy of a crime report, particularly, serious crime (i.e., one of the seven major felonies—murder/non-negligent manslaughter, robbery, forcible rape, burglary, felonious assault, grand larceny, and grand larceny motor vehicle). After Compstat, officers were assigned to make sure every element of the law that defines a particular crime is present before categorizing the complaint as a serious crime. Officers are assigned to call complainants back and ask exactly what happened to be sure each element is present. Also, officers and their supervisors read and re-read complaints to be sure every element of a crime is present. Every attempt is made to classify the complaint as something other than a major felony. There is nothing illegal with this; nevertheless, it is a different way of counting compared to before Compstat where the complainant's word when the report was first taken would essentially be accepted. Thus, by rigidly interpreting applicable laws, commanders can classify complaints into other categories—having the effect of reducing the number of major felonies.

Basically, the consequences of this leadership style (top-down, scientific management approach) are, as Cowper (2000) suggests, dissatisfaction with police in minority communities of New York City, crime reporting problems, and a police force that is combat/enforcement-driven by statistics. While the NYPD is making vast strides to oversee these practices (e.g., they have created a Data Integrity Unit to be sure the entire NYPD is properly counting crime), many police departments that previously emulated Compstat are not. Furthermore, leaders in many of these departments do not understand the ramifications of these policies. There are other negative ramifications of adopting the Compstat process without developing a comprehensive understanding of it.

Aggressive Policing and the Law

From the current findings we can surmise that it may be that very few officers are responsible for the aggressive crime control police work which is considered by some to be the heart of the enormous crime reductions in New York (see, e.g., Bratton 1996; Maple, 1999; Bratton with Knobler, 1999; Kelling and Coles, 1996). This is indicated by the fact that on the questionnaire only a few officers were influenced by Department rewards and punishments. One group of officers who were influenced by these rewards and punishments were anti-crime officers. I think it worth examining their responses to the questionnaire more closely, since they are in a very aggressive crime-fighting unit.

Examining anti-crime officers' responses compared to other officers reveals that anti-crime officers are approximately twice as likely to be illegal in their search/stop decisions (see Table 6.1). Anti-crime officers were sure they would unequivocally do the illegal search in about 28 percent of the cases, while other officers stated they would do the search in only 15 percent of the illegal situations. While the Compstat process is considered successful at reducing crime, there is a concern that officers

Table 6.1
Cross Tabulation: Judgments by Assignment in Three Clearly Illegal Situations*

Judgment	Assignment		
	(1) Anti-crime	(2) Other	Total
Not do the stop	36 (35.0%)	1,259 (52.6%)	1,295 (51.8%)
Unsure	38 (36.9%)	776 (32.4%)	814 (32.6%)
Do the Stop	29 (28.2%)	360 (15.0%)	389 (15.6%)
Total	103 (100.0%)	2,395 (100.0%)	2,498 (100.0%)

*Gamma = −.324, p < .0001 (car stop, weapon search, and drug search situations). Also, percentages may add to more than 100% due to rounding.

who are most aggressive in fighting crime may be the most illegal in their behavior.

The questionnaire also allows us to directly compare responses from officers who indicated they were most aggressive in their attitudes toward crime-fighting with those who were less aggressive, regardless of their assignment. Only 8.8 percent of respondents strongly agreed with the aggressiveness measure that reads, "A good police officer is one who aggressively patrols his/her beat, stopping a number of cars, checking out people, running warrant checks on vehicles that look suspicious and so forth."[11] Of those who strongly agreed with this question, 23.7 percent stated they would unequivocally do an illegal search, compared to 14.4 percent of the less aggressive officers. This roughly 10 percent difference in responses is certainly enough to raise caution flags. That is, those officers who are most aggressive are also those most likely to be illegal in their search/stop behavior. More favorable to aggressive policing is the result which shows that these aggressive officers are also most likely to search when it is clearly legal for officers to do so. Aggressive officers unequivocally searched in 43 percent of the legal situations, whereas less aggressive officers searched in only 35 percent of those situations. Assuming police managers wish to use the aggressive crime-fighting style of Compstat, they need to promote aggressive behavior that leads to increased legal searches/stops by the aggressive officers but, importantly, not get the corresponding illegal searches/stops as seen in the aggressive officers as well. Thus, crime fighting policies are being initiated expeditiously and with bureaucratic efficiency; however, the consequences of these strategies are not fully understood by the public or by many police leaders.

Due Process Policies

We can learn yet another lesson based on Herbert Packer's categorization of crime control versus due process. Jurisdictions replicating Compstat, and those funding the projects, must be exceedingly careful not only to replicate the crime control policies of the New York City Police Department but also to reproduce those policies which focus on due process considerations. In this way aggressive crime control policies are properly balanced by due process policies protecting civil liberties and citizens' rights. Some of these due process policies are newly developed programs, while others reemphasize older programs that were not considered critical in the early stages of Compstat. These would include the Courtesy, Professionalism, and Respect (CPR) program initiated by Police Commissioner Howard Safir; communicating court cases to officers through

Legal Bulletins (or something similar)[12]; using the New York City Police Department's Office of the Deputy Commissioner of Legal Matters as a model; and taking note of some of the relatively recent training efforts by NYPD (e.g., search and seizure training for sergeants and lieutenants). I will explain each of these policies in more detail.

Courtesy, Professionalism, and Respect (CPR)

The CPR strategy was developed by the NYPD by utilizing a complex array of sources. The department took seriously the suggestions, complaints, and comments of policing experts, politicians, and community members. The strategy basically involves the following (NYCPD, 1997a: 4):

> The CPR Strategy is therefore the culmination of internal re-examination, external analysis, and the subsequent recommendations of advisory boards, citizen focus groups, and internal review committees . . . the following components are key to achieving our stated objective:
>
> —Set Professional Standards
> —Revise Recruitment Criteria
> —Incorporate the Philosophy of CPR in All Facets of Training
> —Implement Comprehensive Performance Monitoring
> —Revise Reward and Discipline Systems to Support CPR Goals
> —Expand Public Involvement

Under setting professional standards, the NYPD stresses ideals such as (NYCPD 1997a: 2) "acknowledging the rights and dignity of those we come in contact with; acknowledging the diversity, traditions and cultures of others; being cognizant of the manner in which we speak to others, etc." Recruitment policy focuses "'screening in' desirable candidates rather than 'screening out' unqualified candidates" (NYCPD, 1997a: 4). Under recruitment the CPR program stresses minimum age and education requirements (candidates must be twenty-two and have a least sixty college credits or two years of military experience to be hired).[13] All aspects of training focus on CPR as well.

Monitoring programs were also developed to measure CPR's effectiveness, including random testing of officers and reviewing the Civilian Complaint Review Board (CCRB) statistics at Compstat. This is a very important change in policy, since using CCRB statistics as part of a due process policy is the antithesis of previously emphasized crime-fighting efforts. Importantly, the first full year of the CPR program was 1997, which was also the first year that CCRB complaints began to decrease. Rewards including public recognition of officers, transfers to desired assignments, and giving career advancement points were also initiated. Last, the public was involved in every aspect of these changes. For example, a CCRB mediation program was put in place (i.e., an attempt to mediate CCRB complaints by engaging voluntary participants in frank discussions of incidents). These components of the CPR program address precisely those values which crime control strategies tend to neglect: integrity, valuing human life, and respect for every person. This strategy, then, complements efforts on crime control.

NYPD Legal Bureau

The NYPD's Legal Bureau is a model for other agencies to follow to help ensure that legal matters will be taken seriously by police. The NYPD (2002a) describes the mission of the Legal Bureau thus:

> The mission of the legal bureau is (1) to support the department in preventing crime and reducing fear by assisting its members in interpreting and enforcing state, federal and local laws; (2) to ensure that the policies and practices of the department are lawful and are fairly applied; (3) to develop legislation in accordance with the needs of the department and public safety concerns; (4) to further the quality of life of New York City through the focused and aggressive use of Civil Enforcement remedies.

Particularly relevant to this book is the second mission statement, aimed at ensuring that officers are working within legal guidelines.

To accomplish this mission, the Legal Bureau assists field officers in many ways. One way is by having numerous attorneys on staff who are available to answer questions that may arise. These include questions related to the necessity of a search warrant, the legality of a frisk, and other due process concerns. The Legal Bureau was also responsible for drafting a memo book insert that all police officers are required to carry; it succinctly explains the powers police officers have to stop individuals.

Another way in which the Legal Bureau accomplishes this mission is to issue *Legal Bureau Bulletins* that describe changes in the law as well as court cases which are pertinent to police work. These bulletins summarize the main points of cases as they impact frontline policing. Cases involving car stops, person stops, and searches are commonplace among these bulletins (see example on pages 120–121).[14]

Training Efforts

The New York City Police Academy is a model of training. The NYPD (2002b) describes the duties of the Police Academy thus:

> Maintaining a well-trained Department is the responsibility of the Police Academy. As such, it conducts entry level, in-service, and executive level

training courses. It also prepares lesson plans and new curricula necessary for the Department to meet the demands of the community, crime trends, as well as to be in compliance with new laws. "Enter to Learn Go Forth to Serve" is the Police Academy's slogan. The Police Academy maintains certified police instructors that teach in one of three academic disciplines, Police Science, Law, and Social Science for recruit level training. Physical education as well as firearms and tactics instruction are also part of the recruit training curriculum. Instruction in firearms, tactics, and continuing education are also offered on an on-going basis for in-service and executive level officers. Training is also provided to officers and civilians pertaining to specialized duties, i.e., Emergency Service Unit, investigatory, computer applications, etc. The Police Academy has been striving to be recognized as the "West Point" of law enforcement training academies.

Importantly, this description of the Police Academy indicates that the NYPD does not stop training after recruitment. Rather, training is an integral part of an officer's career. These lessons need to be followed up by supervisors, management, and oversight agencies, so that officers are not receiving conflicting messages (e.g., the Police Academy trains to *legally* conduct stops, whereas field supervisors and other officers train to stop someone on *extralegal* criteria, such as demeanor of the suspect).

Bolstering Compstat

There is room for improvement in the Compstat process both within the NYPD and especially in agencies that have replicated the process. This is based on the fact that police officers are sworn to uphold the Constitution of the United States. This involves much more than crime-fighting. In particular, it also involves protecting due process rights. The NYPD has attempted to address these due process concerns with CPR, an emphasis on its Legal Bureau, and training. Other police agencies should consider these steps, as well as certain aspects of a human relations management approach, and focus training and supervision on legal matters, especially for aggressive crime fighting units.

There is a need, then, to replicate due process programs (i.e., CPR, Legal Bureau, training) when implementing a Compstat process in order to develop a balanced policing approach. Quality of life crackdowns must be thoughtfully and carefully introduced into jurisdictions, keeping a watchful eye on due process rights.

For example, training on the legal restrictions of officers must be vigilant. The data in the questionnaire indicated that some officers were willing to violate restrictions. Although they were relatively few in number, this is troublesome. Lessons should incorporate theory with practical application, especially at entry level. New officers must understand their

NEW YORK CITY POLICE DEPARTMENT

OFFICE OF THE DEPUTY COMMISSIONER - LEGAL MATTERS

LEGAL BUREAU
BULLETIN

| Vol. 24 No. 1 | March, 1994 |

I.   SUBJECT: VEHICLE STOPS

II.   QUESTION: DOES THE USE OF AN RMP'S TURRET LIGHTS, SPOTLIGHT AND/OR LOUDSPEAKER TO DIRECT A VEHICLE TO PULL OVER CONSTITUTE A FORCIBLE STOP?

III.   ANSWER: YES, A VEHICLE STOP UNDER THESE CIRCUMSTANCES AMOUNTS TO A FORCIBLE SEIZURE AND THEREFORE, MUST BE BASED UPON REASONABLE SUSPICION IN ORDER FOR ANY SUBSEQUENT ARREST OR SEIZURE OF EVIDENCE TO BE VALID. *(People v. May, 81 N.Y. 2d 725) (1992).*

IV.   DISCUSSION:

A. FACTS:

Defendant May, and a female companion were seated in a parked car at about 2 a.m. on a deserted street in Manhattan known for illegal drug activity. Two police officers, patrolling in an RMP, drove up behind May's vehicle to investigate. As the officers approached, with the RMP's red turret light and spotlight on, May started the engine of the car and slowly pulled away. After the vehicle had travelled a distance of some 10 or 20 feet, the officers, using the RMP's loudspeaker, ordered May to pull the car over. May immediately complied. Upon approaching the vehicle, the officers noticed that a towel was draped over the steering wheel column. They checked the car's license plate number with the radio dispatcher and were advised that the car was stolen. The officers then placed May under arrest. A search of May's person revealed three (3) vials of crack in his pocket, and when the towel was removed from the steering column the officers discovered that the column had been broken and rewired.

After being indicted for criminal possession of a controlled substance and stolen property, May moved to suppress the crack and the photograph taken of the stolen car, claiming that they were seized unlawfully. The motion was denied and May was convicted. The Appellate Division affirmed the trial court's ruling and May appealed to the New York State Court of Appeals.

B. DECISION:

The Court of Appeals reversed the Appellate Division and trial court's finding that the stop and subsequent arrest of May was justified. The Court granted the defendant's motion to suppress the evidence and dismissed the indictment.

The Court held that when the police, using the RMP's red turret lights, spotlight and loudspeaker, ordered May to pull the car over, the defendant was effectively "seized." Therefore, the stop was justified only if the officers had a reasonable suspicion of illegal activity. The Court found that, under the circumstances of this incident, the officers did not have a reasonable suspicion that a crime had been or was about to be committed. The officers knew only that the defendant and another person were sitting in a car parked on a desolate street, a fact which provided them with no information regarding illegal activity. In addition, the defendant's action in moving the car slowly away as the officers approached did not create a reasonable suspicion of illegal activity. Once the defendant indicated, by pulling away from the curb, that he did not wish to speak with the officers, they had no basis to conduct a forcible stop.

C. ANALYSIS:

The primary problem with this case is that while the officers may have had a basis to approach the vehicle, they had no basis to conduct a forcible stop. Had the officers simply followed the car as it drove away and conducted a computer check of the license to determine if it was stolen, there would have been no constitutional violation. In addition, had the officers been able to approach the car and observe the towel draped over the steering wheel without the need for the use of the RMP's lights, siren or loudspeaker, no "stop" of the vehicle would have occurred.

The result in this case may be easier to understand if you compare the facts here to a person walking down the street. Absent reasonable suspicion of criminal activity, a person may ignore or refuse to answer a police officer's questions and walk away. According to the Court of Appeals, the fact that a person is sitting in a vehicle does not change this rule. The driver of a vehicle, like a person walking down the street, may exercise the right to "walk away" in response to police questioning. The driver, like the pedestrian, may only then be forcibly stopped if there is reasonable suspicion of illegal activity, including a traffic infraction. Developing a basis for the stop of a vehicle may be easier because of the many traffic laws that drivers must obey. However, absent the requisite reasonable suspicion, the driver and the car cannot be directed to pull over.

V. CONCLUSION:

A vehicle stop, accomplished by the use of an RMP's turret lights, siren, spotlight, loudspeaker **or verbal command to pull over,** is a forcible seizure of a motorist. Police officers must have reasonable suspicion of illegal activity to stop a vehicle in this manner. The May case, however, has *not* further limited the instances when the police may stop a vehicle. Vehicles may be stopped under the following circumstances:

(1) You reasonably suspect that the occupant(s) of the vehicle have committed, are committing, or about to commit a crime; or

(2) You have probable cause that the occupant(s) of the vehicle have committed a crime; or

(3) Upon observing the vehicle, you reasonably suspect that a violation of the traffic laws has been committed; or

(4) Upon observing the vehicle, you have probable cause that a violation of the traffic laws has been committed; or

(5) The vehicle is stopped according to some non - arbitrary, non - discretionary, systematic procedure (e.g., a roadblock or DWI checkpoint).

Unless one of the aforementioned circumstances exist, any evidence or contraband obtained as a result of the vehicle stop may be suppressed.

This Legal Bulletin was prepared by,
Sergeant Daniel J. Albano, Attorney,
Legal Bureau

role in the democratic process. Additionally, if officers are more aware of *why* a certain behavior is wanted, they will be more apt to follow directions. This approach may be more successful than an authoritarian dictation of rules.

To properly balance the Compstat process, departments would benefit from telling officers why evidence was suppressed in court or if a case was substantially influenced by officer error, especially in search and seizure or stop and frisk. This would allow officers to learn from their mistakes rather than repeat them over and over. Direct and immediate feedback from other criminal justice agencies (e.g., district attorneys, courts), which has generally been a weakness in the system, would not only allow officers to become familiar with their errors but would also improve supervision. Thus, the department should collect and collate statistics regarding officers' errors in order to identify training needs and address deficiencies.[15]

In addition, on a larger scale there has been some discussion about using decertification as an alternative to typical remedies for Fourth Amendment violations (i.e., exclusionary rule, civil suits, civilian complaints). In many states officers can be decertified (prevented from working as a police officer in the state) for blatant and habitual violation of the rights of suspects (see especially Goldman and Puro, 1987). This needs to be discussed at the state and, more important, at the federal level, as well as with authorities on police (e.g., police chiefs, police commissioners).

In contrast to a police state, officers in the United States have limited powers to fight crime. They must work within the law to enforce the law. Given the results showing aggressive and plainclothes officers are most likely to violate legal restrictions, it is suggested that these officers receive more training and supervision. The NYPD is now much more aware of legal matters compared to the early days of Compstat. Today the NYPD carefully trains its plainclothes officers not simply in proper tactics but also, importantly, in legal matters. Thus, not only are tactics such as properly identifying oneself taught, but the appropriate legal standards required to lawfully stop a suspect are reinforced. For example, as a direct result of the Diallo incident (NYPD shooting of an unarmed black man) in February 1999, the entire Street Crime Unit (an aggressive plainclothes crime-fighting unit) was retrained in legal matters in March 1999. Additionally, there is much more frontline supervision (sergeants and lieutenants) for plainclothes units. The NYPD now takes very seriously legal matters that, in the past, were less critical. Other agencies adopting an aggressive crime-fighting strategy need to balance their Compstat program with due process policies as well.

TERRORISM

To combat terrorism, it will be necessary to expand law enforcement's powers. Part of these expanded powers will undoubtedly be increased authority to stop and search suspects. In New York State, for example, one proposed way to increase police powers to combat terrorism is by legislating a good faith exception to the exclusionary rule (McKinley, 2002). This means that if an officer obtains a search warrant and believes he or she is following all the laws governing search warrants, then even if the warrant is later found to be improper due to a technicality, the evidence obtained on the basis of the search warrant would still be admissible. This good faith exception already exists in many areas of the country as a result of the United States Supreme Court Case *United States v. Leon* (1984). However, in *People v. Bigelow* (1985) the New York State Court of Appeals rejected the good faith exception.

Very aggressive tactics by police and other law enforcement agencies will likely be necessary to prevent future terrorist attacks. Aggressive crime-fighting policies require due process policies to check and balance these expanded powers. Due to the inevitable increase in police power because of the terrorist attacks and threat of future attacks, we as a society must ask how much power law enforcement should be given. This is indeed a difficult question. Certainly law enforcement needs to be given enough power to keep us safe. The amount of power to be conferred will likely increase in proportion to the level of threat as well as future acts of terrorism. This, in turn, means that people will have to give up some of the freedoms they enjoy. This is the essence of the social contract. People give up only so much of their freedom to allow the society to function.

Cesare Beccaria, in his classic work *On Crimes and Punishments* (1764), explains this. Beccaria feels that people are basically rational and that they possess "free will." Paolucci (Beccaria, 1963: xix–xx) explains Beccaria's thoughts on good government and the social contract:

> Political community . . . Beccaria's heart tells him, is, or rather, ought to be the result of an accord entered into by men in order to guarantee for themselves the maximum enjoyment of personal liberty. Each individual willingly sacrifices to the political community only so much of his liberty as "suffices to induce others to defend it." Laws are, or ought to be, simply the necessary conditions of this "social contract."

In the current climate of terrorism, then, people will have to sacrifice more liberty to the political community to guarantee the safety of all. This sacrifice ideally should be willing, so that it conforms to the social contract.

Thus, power will be conferred, but only as much as is necessary to limit the threat to acceptable levels.

However, increasing the power of law enforcement carries with it various risks. One important risk is that if we endow law enforcement with too much power, it may lead to an unlimited government (i.e., a police state). One can easily imagine scores of law enforcement officers asking people for their "papers," reminiscent of Nazi Germany, in the name of fighting terrorism. Other risks are the adverse influence of the police culture during car stops and person stops, and the dangers of aggressive policing.

To help gain the support of the public, to assist in maintaining maximum freedom, and to reduce the risk of unlimited government, the United States should consider bringing together experts in this field (see especially Dershowitz, 2002). Toward that end, the information developed as a result of the research completed for this work will prove useful. Checking and balancing aggressive tactics with due process policies such as CPR, increased legal training, communicating legal decisions and laws, and increased attention to communities will help to offset the increased aggressiveness and powers of law enforcement. Further, clear rules should be composed so that law enforcement is aware of its limitations. Other democracies, such as Great Britain and Israel, where everyday life and democracy go on despite constant acts and the threat of terrorism, should be consulted.

In today's environment of terrorism, if society is to remain free and democratic, then it must endeavor to understand the dynamics of the law with respect to policing. Our very way of life is threatened by terrorism. This threat comes not only from the weapons terrorists have used but also from the fear generated through the threat of their future use or the use of some supposed weapon (e.g., weapons of mass destruction). Most certainly our own distress is a weapon terrorists use against us like a sword pointed at the heart of our democracy. This fear could result in giving too much power to law enforcement, thus threatening to smother the free society that we so deeply cherish. The challenges before us are daunting and the stakes are high. Properly understanding the ramifications of broadening police power is a prerequisite for democratic society to overcome the evils of terrorism.

SUMMARY

The New York City experience with aggressive policing helps to develop a comprehensive understanding of how police officers behave with respect to the law. The damaging influence of the police culture, especially with respect to car and person stops, needs to be addressed. It is recommended that person and car stops be meticulously recorded by police officers to help with supervision. Laws and policies meant to guide police behavior need to be composed carefully, using bright-line rules where possible. The Compstat process, especially in its infancy, overemphasized crime control. Using James Wilson's (1977) categories, Compstat can be described as a legalistic program alienating some communities. Also, Compstat promotes a top-down leadership style based on a scientific management approach that has negative consequences, such as feelings of alienation among the rank and file. Those officers who were most likely to follow the crime control policies of Compstat, aggressive police officers and anti-crime officers, were found to be the most illegal in their behavior.

The NYPD has recognized these issues and developed programs that attempt to balance the crime control policies with due process policies such as Courtesy, Professionalism, and Respect. It is recommended that the numerous other jurisdictions replicating Compstat consider implementing some of these due process policies. Additionally, the use of decertification, now done in many states, so that police officers who blatantly and habitually violate legal guidelines can be prevented from working in another department, could be useful. In today's society, combating terrorism will necessitate increasing police power. These increases need to be checked and balanced with programs to prevent police abuse of these newly imparted powers.

NOTES

1. Officers do not have to report other types of stops, such as merely asking a person what is going on. New York State, for example, has a confusing four-tiered system for police encounters based on the court case *People v. DeBour* (1976). A stop based on reasonable suspicion entitles officers to certain powers that lower-level stops do not allow. For instance, the officer can use force at this level and may be able to frisk and search, depending on the circumstances.

2. Officers may fill out paperwork in exceptional car stop situations, such as when an arrest is made or when a car stop is based on reasonable suspicion that an occupant committed a crime.

3. In the case *People v. Robinson* (2001), the New York Court of Appeals has reviewed *Whren* and New York State has adopted the ruling in *Whren* as well.

4. However, see *Illinois v. Wardlow* (2000) for an opinion in which the Supreme Court rejected bright-line rules.

5. Information on this lecture is at http://law.gsu.edu/sba/docket/miller_lecture.htm.

6. This does not mean that no arrests were made—indeed, many were, but only when the officer in the field felt it appropriate to that situation.

7. Prior NYPD community policing was certainly not a panacea. In fact, there were many problems. For example, officers were empowered to make their own hours, and often took weekends off (when crime was highest). This is not only inappropriate, but also not properly following community policing as taught by the Community Policing Consortium (a partnership of five leading police organizations in the United States: the International Association of Chiefs of Police, the National Organization of Black Law Enforcement Executives, the National Sheriffs' Association, the Police Executive Research Forum, and the Police Foundation).

8. These styles are *not* meant to perfectly explain every nuance of the police department. There are exceptions (programs that may fit into a more service-oriented department) to this basic generalization about the NYPD. However, the styles point out, in general terms, the current emphasis of the NYPD.

9. See Maple (1999) for descriptions of the NYPD as a military model.

10. Police Commissioner William Bratton was largely responsible for the introduction of Compstat. It may be that initially he needed to be very aggressive with commanders and against crime, but even he agrees that this should change over time (see especially Henry, 2000).

11. The wording of this question was developed from a proven instrument utilized by Brown (1981).

12. Heffernan and Lovely (1991) were unable to locate bulletins given to officers on important United States Supreme Court cases in two of the four jurisdictions studied.

13. However, other analyses, not shown, indicated education level did not reduce illegal behavior.

14. Unfortunately many smaller departments cannot afford to have a separate legal person, let alone a legal bureau. Indeed, most departments have so few officers that such a unit would be impractical. However, there is a need for, at a minimum, some legal expertise beyond that of the street officer, especially to perform the duties as stated above, regardless of the size of the agency. States may wish to consider coordinating efforts for several or many jurisdictions to share resources in this area. Smaller jurisdictions might also consider coordinating with surrounding jurisdictions to make this more affordable. In any event, there needs to be a concerted effort to ensure these legal matters are addressed after officers leave the Police Academy.

15. This would include monitoring civil suits.

APPENDIX

Questionnaire Wording

You can create any question administered to officers in the factorial survey by placing the wording which follows from the appropriate dimension into using the basic outline. Officers were given 3 weapon, 3 drug, and 2 ambiguous versus bright-line situations for a total of 8 factorial questions. The levels were chosen randomly by computer. Also, there were attitude and characteristic questions which are found after the wording of the dimensions in this appendix.

BASIC OUTLINE OF VIGNETTE

At roll call the Captain states, [dimension of police organization].
You then go on patrol with your partner in a [dimension of community].
During your tour, and in your sector, you and your partner observe
[dimension of police culture]
[dimension of law].

SPECIFIC WORDING OF LEVELS FOR EACH DIMENSION IN THE FACTORIAL SURVEY

Dimension of Organization

Level 1	"Inspections is in the precinct today."
Level 2	"Civilian complaints have increased."
Level 3	"Have a safe tour."
Level 4	"The precinct is down on felony arrests compared to last year's figures."

Level 5   "Keep your sectors clean today; make arrests where possible. Overtime will be made available for all arrests. Don't be afraid to do your job. As long as your actions are not totally unreasonable, I personally will go to bat for you."

Dimension of Community

Level 1   poor neighborhood
Level 2   wealthy neighborhood

Dimension of Police Culture

Level 1   a cooperative individual
Level 2   a skell
Level 3   a mope who calls you an "asshole"
Level 4   a dirtbag who, two months earlier, was arrested for attacking and injuring three fellow officers

Dimension of Law

Weapon Situation

Level 1   who fits the description of a robbery suspect. He is now sitting in a double parked vehicle along a street known for criminal activity. As you are walking your foot post you approach the car from the passenger side (not the driver's side). No other individuals are in the car. Suddenly, you notice the outline of a gun apparently contained in a brown paper bag right next to the suspect. He seems very nervous and may well grab the gun at any moment. The passenger door is slightly open. Using all appropriate tactics, would you at this time grab the apparent gun in as cautious a manner as possible?

Level 2   who is sitting in a double parked vehicle along a street known for criminal activity. You are walking your foot post and decide to approach the driver to ask him to move the car. No other individuals are in the car. Suddenly, you notice the outline of a gun apparently contained in a brown paper bag right next to the driver's seat. The driver begins to get out of the vehicle but stops upon seeing you. He is now standing with one foot on the pavement and the other in the car as you confront him. Would you at this time grab the apparent gun in as cautious and tactically appropriate manner as possible?

Level 3   who is sitting in a double parked vehicle along a street
                 known for criminal activity. You are walking your foot
                 post and decide to approach the driver to ask him to
                 move the car. No other individuals are in the car. Sud-
                 denly, you notice the outline of a gun apparently con-
                 tained in a brown paper bag on the rear seat on the
                 passenger side (not the driver's side) of the vehicle. The
                 driver begins to get out of the vehicle but stops upon
                 seeing you. He is now standing with one foot on the
                 pavement and the other in the car as you confront him.
                 Would you at this time grab the apparent gun in as cau-
                 tious and tactically appropriate manner as possible?

Level 4   who double parks a vehicle along a street you are walk-
                 ing on. The driver then gets out and casually walks to an
                 apartment building to ring a doorbell. You are walking
                 your foot post and as you approach the car you notice
                 the outline of a gun apparently contained in a brown
                 paper bag on the passenger seat of the locked car. No one
                 is in the car. Assuming you know a way to get in the car
                 quickly and without damaging it, would you at this time
                 grab the apparent gun in as cautious and tactically appro-
                 priate manner as possible?

Drug Situation

Level 1   who you know to be a drug dealer. He places what ap-
                 pears to be 100 marijuana cigarettes into an unlocked
                 duffel bag. You immediately arrest the suspect who is
                 holding the zippered shut duffel bag in his hand on a
                 crowded street corner. You realize that the bag could
                 easily be destroyed by throwing it into a nearby fire in a
                 garbage can. Immediately, fearing destruction of the evi-
                 dence, you take the bag from his hand. Would you with-
                 out delay, at the arrest site and in the presence of the
                 arrestee, look inside the unlocked duffel bag?

Level 2   who you know to be a drug dealer. He places what ap-
                 pears to be 100 marijuana cigarettes into a duffel bag.
                 You immediately arrest the suspect who has the zippered
                 shut duffel bag on the ground between his legs. Imme-
                 diately, you seize the duffel bag. Would you at the ar-
                 rest site and in the presence of the arrestee, look inside
                 the duffel bag?

Level 3   who you have never seen before. He places what appears
               to be 100 marijuana cigarettes into a locked duffel bag.
               You immediately arrest and handcuff the suspect with two
               other officers. The suspect has the duffel bag, which is
               now locked shut, on the ground between his legs. You
               find the key to the bag in the right pants pocket of the
               arrested individual. Would you at the arrest site and in the
               presence of the arrestee, open and look inside the duffel
               bag?

Level 4   who you have never seen before. He places what appears
               to be 100 marijuana cigarettes into a securely locked
               briefcase. You immediately arrest the suspect who now has
               the locked shut briefcase on the ground between his legs.
               You frisk the suspect with several other officers present
               leaving the briefcase on the ground. No key is found for
               the briefcase. Would you, at the arrest site and in the pres-
               ence of the arrestee, force open and look inside the brief-
               case?

Person Stop

Level 1   a man who is standing with two others on a street cor-
               ner. As soon as you (dressed in full uniform) get close to
               him, he suddenly, without warning, nervously turns and
               starts running. Would you run after this person?

Car Stop

Level 2   who you recognize from a past encounter, driving by in
               a vehicle. Assuming you are in an RMP, would you stop
               the vehicle in order to check the person's operators license
               and vehicle registration?

Instructions: Please circle the choice that describes your feelings toward
each of the following statements.*

---

*Questions one and two are reproduced from Table A.1 in *Working the Street:
Police Discretion and the Dilemmas of Reform*, by Michael K. Brown ©1981 Russell
Sage Foundation, 112 East 64th Street, New York, NY 10021. Reprinted with
permisssion.

(1) A good police officer is one who aggressively patrols his/her beat, stopping a number of cars, checking out people, running warrant checks on vehicles that look suspicious, and so forth.

| Strongly Agree | Somewhat Agree | Somewhat Disagree | Strongly Disagree |

(2) A police officer should not make a lot of arrests for minor violations or issue a lot of citations for minor traffic infractions.

| Strongly Agree | Somewhat Agree | Somewhat Disagree | Strongly Disagree |

(3) Police officers _____ fail to take necessary action due to a feeling that supervisors will disapprove of their actions.

| Often | Sometimes | Rarely | Never |

(4) _____ people in the community you work in respect police officers.

| Most | Some | Few | Very few |

(5) Officers in my precinct respect an officer who makes a lot of collars.

| Strongly Agree | Somewhat Agree | Somewhat Disagree | Strongly Disagree |

(6) Making many arrests will _____ my chances to advance my career.

| greatly | slightly | slightly | greatly |

(7) Rate the following statements on a scale of 0 to 100, 0 being not important at all to you and 100 being of the utmost importance to you. DO NOT USE THE SAME NUMBER TWO TIMES (NO TIES). Officers should:

be honest _____
know citizens in the precinct _____
be vigilant in enforcing the law _____
be concerned about citizens' "well-being" _____
protect civil liberties _____

THE FOLLOWING QUESTIONS ARE FOR STATISTICAL PURPOSES ONLY

1. What is your gender? (Circle one)

   Male   Female

2. How old are you? (to the nearest full year, e.g., 25, 35, etc.)

   _____ years old.

3. What is your specific assignment? (e.g., RMP; Steady foot post; Highway safety officer; RIP; anti-crime).

   _____

4. How many years have you been a police officer? (to the nearest full year, e.g., 1, 5, 30, etc.)

   _____ years.

5. What is your educational level? DO **NOT** INCLUDE POLICE ACADEMY CREDITS.
   (Circle only one)

   High school equivalency (G.E.D.)

   High school diploma

   Up to 24 college credits

   Between 25 and 48 college credits

   Between 49 and 72 college credits (including Associate's)

   72 or more college credits

   Bachelor's degree

   Work toward Master's degree

   Master's degree or more

   Legal degree (e.g., J.D.)

6. Make any other comments about this survey below. (Use back of sheet if necessary.)

References

BIBLIOGRAPHY

The Academic American Encyclopedia. (1996). Grolier Multimedia Encyclopedia Version. Danbury, CT: Grolier.

Alderson, John. (1979). *Policing Freedom: A Commentary on the Dilemmas of Policing Western Democracies.* Plymouth, UK: Latimer Trend.

Alschuler, Albert W. (1984). "Bright Line Fever and the Fourth Amendment." *University of Pittsburgh Law Review* 45: 227–288.

Amsterdam, Anthony G. (1974). "Perspectives on the Fourth Amendment." *Minnesota Law Review* 58: 349–439.

Andrews, W. (1995). "The New NYPD." *Spring 3100* 58, no. 3/4: 44–45.

Armstrong, Terry R., and Kenneth M. Cinnamon, eds. (1976). *Power and Authority in Law Enforcement.* Springfield, IL: Charles C. Thomas.

Atkinson, David S. (1985). "The Supreme Court and the Police: Constitutional Searches and Seizures." In Blumberg and Niederhoffer (1985): 258–266.

Attorney General, State of New York, Eliot Spitzer. (1999). "A Report to the People of the State of New York from the Office of the Attorney General." New York.

Babbie, Earl. (1989). *The Practice of Social Research.* 5th ed. Belmont, CA: Wadsworth.

Barry, Dan. (1997). "12 in Brooklyn Precinct Reassigned in Abuse Inquiry: Mayor Demands Other Officers Cooperate." *New York Times,* August 15: A1.

Baum, Lawrence. (1985). *The Supreme Court.* 2nd ed. Washington, DC: Congressional Quarterly.

Bayley, David H. (1994). *Police for the Future.* New York: Oxford University Press.

Bayley, David H. (1986). "The Tactical Choices of Police Patrol Officers." *Journal of Criminal Justice* 14: 329–348.

Bayley, David H., and Egon Bittner. (1984). "Learning the Skills of Policing." In Dunham and Alpert (1993): 106–129.

Beccaria, Cesare. (1963) [1764]. *On Crimes and Punishments*. Translated with an introduction by Henry Paolucci. New York: Macmillan.

Bittner, Egon. (1974). "Florence Nightingale in Pursuit of Willie Sutton: A Theory of Police." In Herbert Jacob (ed.), *The Potential for Reform of Criminal Justice*. Beverly Hills, CA: Sage.

Bittner, Egon. (1970). "The Police Charge." Reprinted in Lundman (1980): 28–42. From Egon Bittner, "The Functions of the Police in Modern Society." *National Institute of Mental Health*: 36–47.

Black, Donald. (1970). "Production of Crime Rates." *American Sociological Review* 35: 735–748.

Black's Law Dictionary. (1979). 5th ed. St. Paul, MN: West.

Blumberg, Abraham S., and Elaine Niederhoffer. (1985) [1976]. *The Ambivalent Force*. 3rd ed. New York: Holt, Rinehart and Winston.

Bohrnstedt, George W. "Measurement." In Rossi, Wright, and Anderson (1983): 69–121.

Bouza, Anthony V. (1990). *The Police Mystique: An Insider's Look at Cops, Crime, and the Criminal Justice System*. New York: Plenum Press.

Bradburn, Norman M. (1983). "Response Effects." In Rossi et al. (1983): 289–328.

Bratton, William J. (1996). "Great Expectations: How Higher Expectations for Police Departments Can Lead to a Decrease in Crime." Unpublished paper.

Bratton, William, with Peter Knobler. (1999). *Turnaround: How America's Top Cop Reversed the Crime Epidemic*. New York: Random House.

Brooks, Laure Weber. (1993). "Police Discretionary Behavior: A Study of Style." In Dunham and Alpert (1993): 140–164.

Brown, Michael K. (1981). *Working the Street*. New York: Russell Sage Foundation.

Burleigh, Michael, and Wolfgang Wipperman. (1991). *The Racial State: Germany 1933–1945*. Melbourne, Australia: Cambridge University Press.

Burton, Velmer S., Jr., James Frank, Robert H. Langworthy, and Troy A. Barder. (1993). "The Prescribed Roles of Police in a Free Society: Analyzing State Legal Codes." *Justice Quarterly* 10, no. 4: 683–695.

Butterfoss, Edwin J. (1988). "Bright Line Seizures: The Need for Clarity in Determining When Fourth Amendment Activity Begins." *Journal of Criminal Law and Criminology* 79, no. 2: 437–482.

Canon, Bradley. (1979). "The Exclusionary Rule: Have Critics Proven That It Doesn't Deter Police?" *Judicature* 62, no. 8 (March): 398–403.

Chambliss, William. (1994). "Policing the Ghetto Underclass: The Politics of Law and Law Enforcement." *Social Problems* 41, no. 2: 177–194.

Chevigny, Paul. (1969). *Police Power: Police Abuses in New York City*. New York: Pantheon Books.

Clymer, Adam. (2001). "Bush Quickly Signs Measure Aiding Antiterrorism Effort." *New York Times*, October 27: B5.

Columbia Law School. (1968). "Effect of *Mapp v. Ohio* on Police Search-and-Seizure Practices in Narcotics Cases." *Columbia Journal of Law and Social Problems* 4: 87–104.

Cooper, Michael. (1997). "Error Prompts Review Board to Take Steps." *New York Times,* December 12: B3.

Cowper, Thomas J. (2000). "The Myth of the 'Military Model' of Leadership in Law Enforcement." *Police Quarterly* 3, no. 3: 228–246.

Crank, John P. (1995). "Understanding Police Culture." Unpublished paper presented at the Annual Meeting of the Academy of Criminal Justice Sciences, March 7–11, Boston.

Dao, James. (1996). "Pataki Gains Pick as Court Loses Judge." *New York Times,* April 6: Metro 28.

Davies, Thomas Y. (1983). "A Hard Look at What We Know (and Still Need to Learn) About the 'Costs' of the Exclusionary Rule: The NIJ Study and Other Studies of 'Lost' Arrests." *American Bar Foundation Research Journal* no. 3: 611–690.

Davies, Thomas Y. (1974). "Critique on the Limitations of Empirical Evaluations of the Exclusionary Rule: A Critique of the Spiotto Research and United States v. Calandra." *Northwestern University School of Law* 69, no. 5: 740–798.

Davis, Kenneth Culp. (1975). *Police Discretion.* St. Paul, MN: West.

Delattre, Edwin J. (1994). *Character and Cops: Ethics in Policing.* 2nd ed. Washington, DC: American Enterprise Institute.

Dershowitz, Alan M. (2002). *Shouting Fire: Civil Liberties in a Turbulent Age.* Boston: Little, Brown.

Dershowitz, Alan M. (1996). *Reasonable Doubts.* New York: Simon and Schuster.

Dictionary of Crime: Criminal Justice, Criminology and Law Enforcement. (1992). Jay Robert Nash, ed. (New York: Paragon House).

Dillman, Don A. (1983). "Mail and Other Self-Administered Questionnaires." In Rossi et al. (1983): 359–377.

Dixon, David. (1997). *Law in Policing: Legal Regulation and Police Practices.* Oxford: Clarendon.

Douglas, William O. (1954). *An Almanac of Liberty* (Garden City, NY: Doubleday). Quoted in James B. Simpson (1992). *Webster's II: New Riverside Desk Quotations.* Boston: Houghton Mifflin.

Drew, Christopher, and Judith Miller. (2002). "Though Not Linked to Terrorism, Many Detainees Cannot Go Home." *New York Times,* February 18: A1, A9.

Drummond, Douglas S. (1976). *Police Culture.* Beverly Hills, CA: Sage.

Dunham, Roger G., and Geoffrey P. Alpert, eds. (1993). *Critical Issues in Policing.* 2nd ed. Prospect Heights, IL: Waveland Press.

Dworkin, Roger B. (1973). "Fact Style Adjudication and the Fourth Amendment: The Limits of Lawyering." *Indiana Law Journal* (spring): 329–368.

Eterno, John A. (2001). "Zero Tolerance Policing in Democracies: The Dilemma of Controlling Crime Without Increasing Police Abuse of Power." *Police Practice and Research* 2, no. 3: 189–217.

Fairfield, Roy. (1976). "The Paradox of Power." In Armstrong and Cinnamon (1976): 13–22.

Federal Bureau of Investigation. *Crime in the United States: Uniform Crime Reports.* Washington, DC: U.S. Government Printing Office.

Fielding, Nigel G. (1989). "Police Culture and Police Practice." In Mollie Weatheritt, ed. (1989). *Police Research: Some Future Prospects.* Brookfield, VT: Gower.

Flynn, Kevin. 2000. "Behind the Success Story, a Vulnerable Police Force." *New York Times,* November 28: A1.

"For Police Union Head, Review Board Proposal Is Latest Indignity." *New York Times,* June 28: L25.

Fyfe, James J., David A. Klinger, and Jeanne M. Flavin. (1997). "Differential Police Treatment of Male-on-Female Spousal Violence." *Criminology* 35, no. 3: 455–473.

Galliher, John F. (1971). "Explanations of Police Behavior: A Critical Review and Analysis." In Niederhoffer and Blumberg (1976): 64–71.

Gangi, Robert. (1997). "Why Is City Crime Going Down? It's the Demographics, Stupid." *New York Daily News,* January 14.

Glaberson, William. (2001). "Support for Bush's Antiterror Plan." *New York Times,* December 5: B6.

Goldman, Roger, and Steven Puro. (1987). "Decertification of Police: An Alternative to Traditional Remedies for Police Misconduct." *Hastings Constitutional Law Quarterly* 15, no. 7: 45–80.

Goldstein, Herman. (1977). *Policing a Free Society.* Cambridge, MA: Balinger.

Goldstein, Joseph. (1992). *The Intelligible Constitution: The Supreme Court's Obligation to Maintain the Constitution as Something We the People Can Understand.* New York: Oxford University Press.

Goldstein, Joseph. (1984). "Police Discretion Not to Invoke the Criminal Process: Low-Visibility Decisions in the Administration of Justice." *The Yale Law Journal* 69: 543–594.

"The Governor's Attack on the Judges." (1996). *New York Times,* February 3: A22.

Grano, Joseph D. (1982). "Rethinking the Fourth Amendment Warrant Requirement." *American Criminal Law Review* 19, no. 3 (Winter): 603–650.

Greene, Judith. (1999). "Zero Tolerance: A Case Study of Police Policies and Practices in New York City." *Crime and Delinquency* 45, no. 2: 171–187.

Greenhouse, Linda. (2001). Pulitzer Prize-winning *New York Times* reporter's lecture. Cited at http://law.gsu.edu/sba/docket/miller_lecture.htm.

Haberman, Clyde. (1997). "Civil Tones on a Topic of Violence." *New York Times,* September 12: B1.

Haberman, Clyde (1996). "State Courts Found Guilty By Jury of Peers." *New York Times.* March 8: B1.

Heffernan, William C. (1989). "On Justifying Fourth Amendment Exclusion." *Wisconsin Law Review* 1989: 1193–1154.

Heffernan, William C., and Richard W. Lovely. (1991). "Evaluating the Fourth Amendment Exclusionary Rule: The Problem of Police Compliance with the Law." *University of Michigan Journal of Law Reform* 24: 311–369.

Henry, Vincent E. (2000). "Interview with William J. Bratton." *Police Practice and Research: An International Journal* 2, no. 4: 559–580.

Hirschel, Joseph D. (1977). "Searching for Reasonable Protection of Fourth Amendment Rights: The Exclusionary Rule and Its Alternates." Ph.D. dissertation, SUNY Albany. Ann Arbor, MI: University Microfilms.

Howard, Philip K. (1994). *The Death of Common Sense: How Law is Suffocating America.* New York: Warner Books.

Israel, Jerold H., and Wayne R. LaFave. (1988). *Criminal Procedure.* 4th ed. St. Paul, MN: West.

Johnson, Charles A., and Bradley C. Canon. (1984). *Judicial Policies: Implementation and Impact.* Washington, DC: Congressional Quarterly.

Kamisar, Yale. (1990). "Remembering the 'Old World' of Criminal Procedure: A Reply to Professor Grano." *University of Michigan Journal of Law Reform* 22: 537–589.

Kamisar, Yale. (1979). "The Exclusionary Rule in Historical Perspective: The Struggle to Make the Fourth Amendment More Than 'an Empty Blessing.'" *Judicature* 62, no. 7 (February): 337–350.

Kamisar, Yale, Wayne R. LaFave, and Jerold H. Israel. (1990). *Modern Criminal Procedure: Cases, Comments and Questions.* St. Paul, MN: West.

Kaplan, John. (1974). "The Limits of the Exclusionary Rule." *Stanford Law Review* 26:1027–1055.

Kelling, George. (1999). "'Broken Windows' and Police Discretion." *National Institute of Justice Research Report* (October): 1.

Kelling, George L., and Catherine M. Coles. (1996). *Fixing Broken Windows: Restoring Order and Reducing Crime in Our Communities.* New York: The Free Press.

Kelly, Alfred H., Winfred A. Harbison, and Herman Belz. (1983). *The American Constitution: Its Origins and Development.* New York: W. W. Norton.

Klinger, David A. (1994). "Demeanor or Crime? Why 'Hostile' Citizens Are More Likely to Be Arrested." *Criminology* 32, no. 3 (August): 475–493.

Klotter, John C., and Jacqueline R. Kanovitz (1983). *Constitutional Law.* Cincinnati, OH: W. H. Anderson.

Krauss, Clifford. (1996). "Fighting Police Corruption." *New York Times,* March 4: B1.

Krauss, Clifford. (1995a). "The Commissioner vs. the Criminologists." *New York Times,* November 11: Metro 43.

Krauss, Clifford. (1995b). "Officers' Training Moves to the Streets." *New York Times,* November 12: 41, 45.

LaFave, Wayne R. (1993). "Police Rule Making and the Fourth Amendment: The Role of the Courts." In Ohlin and Remington (1993): 211–277.

LaFave, Wayne R. (1974). "'Case-by-Case Adjudication' Versus 'Standardized Procedures': The Robinson Dilemma." *Supreme Court Review:* 127–163.

LaFave, Wayne R. (1972). "Warrantless Searches and the Supreme Court—Further Ventures into the Quagmire." *Criminal Law Bulletin* 8, no. 1 (January/February): 9–30.

Leadership for the Transition to Community Policing Participant's Guide. (2001). Washington, D.C.: Community Policing Consortium.

Levy, Clifford J. (1996). "Pataki Is Seeking Curbing of Rights of Crime Suspects." *New York Times,* January 30: A1.

Loewenthal, Milton A. (1980). "Evaluating the Exclusionary Rule in Search and Seizure." *UMKC Law Review* 49: 24–40.

Lundman, Richard J. (1994). "Demeanor or Crime? The Midwest City Police-Citizen Encounters Study." *Criminology* 32, no. 4: 631–653.

Lundman, Richard J. (1980). *Police Behavior: A Sociological Perspective.* New York: Oxford University Press.

Lundman, Richard J. (1974). "Routine Police Arrest Practices: A Commonweal Perspective." *Social Problems* 22: 128–141. Reprinted in Lundman (1980): 182–200.

Lynch, Michael J., and W. Byron Groves. (1989). *A Primer in Radical Criminology.* New York: Harrow and Heston.

McCoy, C. (1985). "Lawsuits Against Police—What Impact Do They Really Have?" Cited in J. J. Fyfe (ed). (1985). *Legal Guide for Police: Constitutional Issues.* Cincinnati, OH: Anderson.

McElroy, Jerome E., and Herman Goldstein. (1992). "Edgy Police, Suspicious Civilians." *New York Times,* October 23: A33.

McKinley, James C., Jr. (2002). "Bill Would Broaden Powers of Police to Fight Terrorism." *New York Times,* June 14: B9.

Manning, Peter K. (1987). "The Police Occupational Culture in Anglo-American Societies." Draft, March 3,1987. Intended for William G. Bailey ed. (1989), *Encyclopedia of Police Science.* Dallas: Garland.

Manning, Peter K. (1978). "The Police: Mandate, Strategies, and Appearances." In Manning and Van Maanen (1978): 7–31.

Manning, Peter K. (1977). *Police Work: The Social Organization of Policing.* Cambridge, MA: MIT Press.

Manning, Peter K., and John Van Maanen. (1978). *Policing: A View From the Street.* Santa Monica, CA: Goodyear Publishing Company, Inc.

Maple, Jack (1999). *The Crime Fighter: Putting the Bad Guys Out of Business.* New York: Doubleday.

Marzulli, John. (2001). "New Stop, Frisk Rule for NYPD." *New York Daily News,* January 4: 2.

Mastrofski, Stephen D, and R. Richard Ritti. (1993). "You Can Lead a Horse to Water . . . : A Case Study of a Police Department's Response to Stricter Drunk-Driving Laws." *Justice Quarterly* 9, no. 3 (September): 465–491.

Mastrofski, Stephen D., Robert E. Worden, and Jeffrey B. Snipes. (1995). "Law Enforcement in a Time of Community Policing." *Criminology* 33, no. 4: 539–563.

Meadows, R. J., and L. C. Trostle (1988). "A Study of Police Misconduct and Litigation: Findings and Implications." *Journal of Contemporary Criminal Justice* 4: 77–82.

Nardulli, Peter F. (1992). *The Constitution and American Political Development.* Chicago, IL: University of Illinois Press.

Nardulli, Peter F. (1983). "The Societal Cost of the Exclusionary Rule: An Empirical Assessment." *American Bar Foundation Research Journal* 3: 585–609.

Nevins, Allan, and Henry Steele Commager. (1986). *A Pocket History of the United States.* New York: Washington Square Press.

New York City Civilian Complaint Review Board. (2000). "Civilian Complaint Review Board Status Report January–December 2000." 8, no. 2.

New York City Civilian Complaint Review Board. (2001). "Street Stop Encounter Report: An Analysis of CCRB Complaints Resulting from the New York Police Department's 'Stop and Frisk' Practices." (June). CCRB website, www.nyc.gov/html/ccrb/home.html.

New York City Police Department. (2002a). Description of Legal Bureau. www.ci.nyc.ny.us/html/nypd/html/dclm/legbur.html.

New York City Police Department. (2002b). Description of Police Academy. www.ci.nyc.ny.us/html/nypd/html/chfpers/pa.html.

New York City Police Department. (2000). "NYPD Response to the Draft Report of the United States Commission on Civil Rights—Police Practices and Civil Rights in New York City." Press release, May 16.

New York City Police Department. (1999). "Police Commissioner Safir Comments on State Attorney General's *Stop and Frisk* Report." Press release, November 30.

New York City Police Department (1998). "The Compstat Process." Unpublished material explaining Compstat.

New York City Police Department. (1997a). "Courtesy, Professionalism, and Respect." Unpublished pamphlet explaining the program.

New York City Police Department. (1997b). "Police Student's Guide—Law." Unpublished student guide for recruit training in law.

New York City Police Department. (1997c). "Police Student's Guide—Police Science." Unpublished student guide for training in police science.

New York City Police Department. *Legal Bureau Bulletins.* Official material disseminated by the Office of the Deputy Commissioner, Legal Matters, to New York City police officers stating policy on legal issues.

Niederhoffer, Elaine, and Abraham S. Blumberg. (1976). *The Ambivalent Force.* New York: Holt, Rinehart and Winston.

Oaks, Dallin H. (1970). "Studying the Exclusionary Rule in Search and Seizure." *The University of Chicago Law Review* 37: 665–756.

O'Brien, David M. (1993). *Supreme Court Watch—1993.* New York: W. W. Norton.

Ohlin, Lloyd E., and Frank J. Remington (eds.). (1993). *Discretion in Criminal Justice: The Tension Between Individualization and Uniformity.* Albany: State University of New York Press.

Orfield, Myron W., Jr. (1987). "The Exclusionary Rule and Deterrence: An Empirical Study of Chicago Narcotics Officers." *University of Chicago Law Review* 54: 1016–1069.

Packer, Herbert. (1966). "The Courts, the Police, and the Rest of Us." *Journal of Criminal Law and Criminology* 57: 238–240.

Paolucci, Henry. (1963). Introduction to Beccaria (1963): xix–xx.

Prottas, Jeffrey M. (1978). "The Power of the Street-Level Bureaucrat in Public Service Bureaucracies." *Urban Affairs Quarterly* 13, no. 3: 285–312.

Purdy, Matthew. (1997). "In New York, the Handcuffs Are One-Size-Fits-All." *New York Times,* August 24: A1.

Purpura, Philip P. (1997). *Criminal Justice: An Introduction.* Newton, MA: Butterworth-Heinemann.

Ramirez, Deborah, Jack McDevitt, and Amy Farrell. (2000). *A Resource Guide on Racial Profiling Data Collection Systems: Promising Practices and Lessons Learned.* Washington, DC: National Institute of Justice.

Rashbaum, William K. (1996). "Complaints Against Cops Surge 135%." *New York Daily News,* April 23: 22.

Rayner, R. (1995). "Wanted: A Kinder, Gentler Cop." *New York Times Magazine,* January 22: 26.

Reiman, Jeffrey. (1990). *The Rich Get Richer and the Poor Get Prison: Ideology, Class, and Criminal Justice.* New York: Macmillan Publishing.

Reinharz, Peter. (1996). "The Court Criminals Love." *City Journal* (winter) 6, no. 1: 38–48.

Reiss, Albert J., Jr. (1971). *The Police and the Public.* New Haven, CT: Yale University Press: 156, 160–163, 170–171. Reprinted in Lundman (1980): 253–259.

Reuss-Ianni, Elizabeth. (1983). *Two Cultures of Policing.* New Brunswick, NJ: Transaction Books.

Riksheim, Eric C., and Steven M. Chermak. (1993). "Causes of Police Behavior Revisited." *Journal of Criminal Justice* 21, no. 4: 353–382.

Rohde, David. (1998). "$76 Million for Man Shot by the Police." *New York Times,* April 9: B6.

Rossi, Peter H., and Steven L. Nock. (1982). *Measuring Social Judgments.* Beverly Hills, CA: Sage.

Rossi, Peter, James Wright, and Andy Anderson (eds.). (1983). *Handbook of Survey Research.* New York: Academic Press.

Rothwax, Harold J. (1996). *Guilty: The Collapse of Criminal Justice.* New York: Random House.

Rubinstein, Jonathan. (1973). *City Police.* New York: Ballantine Books.

Schaefer, Richard T. (2001). *Sociology.* 7th ed. New York: McGraw-Hill.

Schmalleger, Frank. (1995). *Criminal Justice Today: An Introductory Text for the Twenty-first Century.* Englewood Cliffs, NJ: Prentice-Hall.

Schrock, Thomas S., and Robert C. Welsh. (1974). "Up from Calandra: The Exclusionary Rule as a Constitutional Requirement." *Minnesota Law Review* 59: 251–383.

Segal, Jeffrey A., and Harold J. Spaeth. (1993). *The Supreme Court and the Attitudinal Model.* New York: Cambridge University Press.

Sengupta, Somini. (2002). "India Passes Antiterror Bill over Protests About Rights." *New York Times,* March 27: A5.

Shepard, Robin Engel, Jennifer M. Calnon, and Thomas J. Bernard. (2002). "Theory and Racial Profiling: Shortcomings and Future Directions in Research." *Justice Quarterly* 19, no. 2: 249–274.

Silverman, Eli B. (1999). *NYPD Battles Crime: Innovative Strategies in Policing.* Boston: Northeastern University Press.

Silverman, Eli B. (1997). "Why is city crime going down? Give cops most of the credit." *New York Daily News,* January 14.

Simon, James F. (1995). *The Center Holds.* New York: Simon and Schuster.

Simpson, James B. (1992). *Webster's II: New Riverside Desk Quotations.* Boston: Houghton Mifflin.

Skolnick, Jerome. (1966). *Justice Without Trial: Law Enforcement in Democratic Society.* New York: John Wiley and Sons.

Skolnick, Jerome, and James J. Fyfe. (1993). *Above the Law.* New York: The Free Press.

Sontag, Deborah, and Dan Barry. (1997). "Police Complaints Settled, Rarely Resolved." *New York Times,* September 17: A1, B5.

Spiotto, James E. (1973). "Search and Seizure: An Empirical Study of the Exclusionary Rule and Its Alternatives." *Journal of Legal Studies* 2: 243–278.

Stoddard, Ellwyn R. (1968). "The Informal 'Code' of Police Deviancy: A Group Approach to Blue-Coat Crime." *Journal of Criminal Law, Criminology and Police Science* 59: 201–213. Reprinted in Lundman (1980): 226–253.

Sutton, Paul. (1986). "The Fourth Amendment in Action: An Empirical Review of the Search Warrant Process." *Criminal Law Bulletin* 22, no. 5: 405–429.

Sykes, Richard E., and John P. Clark. (1975). "A Theory of Deference Exchange in Police-Civilian Encounters." *American Journal of Sociology* 81: 587–595. Reprinted in Lundman (1980): 91–105.

Tennenbaum, Abraham N. (1994). "The Influence of the *Garner* Decision on Police Use of Deadly Force." *The Journal of Criminal Law & Criminology* 85, no. 1: 241–260.

Toner, Robin, and Janet Elder. (2001). "Public Is Wary but Supportive on Rights Curbs." *New York Times,* December 12: A1.

Uchida, Craig D., and Timothy S. Bynum. (1991). "Search Warrants, Motions to Suppress and 'Lost Cases': The Effects of the Exclusionary Rule in Seven Jurisdictions." *The Journal of Criminal Law and Criminology* 81, no. 4: 1034–1066.

Van Maanen, John. (1978). "The Asshole." Reprinted in Manning and Van Maanen (1978): 228–238. Also reprinted in Lundman (1980): 296–311.

Vold, George B., and Thomas J. Bernard. (1986). *Theoretical Criminology.* New York: Oxford University Press.

Vorenberg, James. (1976). "Narrowing the Discretion of Criminal Justice Officials." *Duke Law Journal* 1976, no. 4:651–697.

Warren, Earl. (1959). "Unanimous Opinion That Confessions Obtained Under Duress Must Be Excluded from Criminal Proceedings." Cited in James B. Simpson. (1992). *Webster's II: New Riverside Desk Quotations.* Boston: Houghton Mifflin.

Westley, William A. (1970). *Violence and the Police: A Sociological Study of Law, Custom, and Morality.* Cambridge, MA: MIT Press.

Whitebread, Charles H. (1985). "The Burger Court's Counterrevolution in Criminal Procedure: The Recent Criminal Decisions of the United States Supreme Court." *Washburn L.J.* 24: 471–485.

Wilkey, Malcolm Richard. (1982). "The Exclusionary Rule: Costs and Viable Alternatives." *Criminal Justice Ethics* 1 (summer/fall): 16–27.

Wilson, Bradford. (1983). "Enforcing the Fourth Amendment: The Original Understanding." *Catholic Lawyer* 28 (summer): 173–198.

Wilson, James Q. (1977). *Varieties of Police Behavior.* Cambridge, MA: Harvard University Press.

Worden, Robert E. (1992a). "Police Officers' Belief Systems: A Framework for Analysis." Unpublished paper presented at the Annual Meeting of the American Political Science Association, August 29–September 1, 1985, New Orleans, LA, and the Annual Meeting of the Academy of Criminal Justice Sciences, March 10–14, 1992, Pittsburgh, PA.

Worden, Robert E. (1992b). "The 'Causes' of Police Brutality." Draft for William A. Geller and Hans Toch, eds. (1996). *Police Violence: Understanding and Controlling Police Abuse of Force.* New Haven, CT: Yale University Press.

Worden, Robert E., and Robin L. Shepard. (1996). "Demeanor, Crime, and Police Behavior: A Reexamination of the Police Services Study Data." *Criminology* 34, no. 1: 83–105.

CASES CITED

Andresen v. Maryland 427 U.S. 463 (1976)
Bigelow, People v. 66 N.Y. 2d 417 (1985)
Boyd v. United States 116 U.S. 616 (1886)
Brown v. Board of Education of Topeka 347 U.S. 483 (1954)
Brown v. Board of Education of Topeka 349 U.S. 294 (1955)
California v. Acevedo 500 U.S. 565 (1991)
California v. Greenwood 486 U.S. 35 (1988)
California v. Hodari D. 111 S. Ct. 1547 (1991)
Cantor, People v. 36 N.Y. 2d 106 (1975)
Carvey, People v. 89 N.Y. 2d 707 (1997)
Chapman v. United States 365 U.S. 610 (1961)
Chimel v. California 395 U.S. 752 (1969)
Colorado v. Bertine 479 U.S. 367 (1987)
DeBour, People v. 40 N.Y. 2d 210 (1976)
Defore, People v. 242 N.Y. 13, 150 N.E. 585 (1926)
Delaware v. Prouse 440 U.S. 648 (1979)
Diaz, People v. 81 N.Y. 2d 106 (1993)
Dred Scott v. Sanford 60 U.S. 393 (1857)
Dunaway v. New York 442 U.S. 200 (1979)
Dunn, People v. 77 N.Y. 2d 19 (1990)
Elkins v. United States 364 U.S. 206 (1960)

Florida v. J.L. 529 U.S. 266 (2000)
Florida v. Riley 488 U.S. 445 (1989)
Galak, People v. 81 N.Y. 2d 463 (1993)
Gokey, People v. 469 N.Y.S. 2d 618 (Ct. App. 1983)
Illinois v. Wardlow 528 U.S. 119 (2000)
Jackson, People v. 79 N.Y. 2d 907 (1992)
Katz v. United States 389 U.S. 347 (1967)
Leon, United States v. 468 U.S. 897 (1984)
Love, People v. 84 N.Y. 2d 917 (1994)
Mapp v. Ohio 367 U.S. 643 (1961)
Martinez, People v. 80 N.Y. 2d 444 (1992)
Minnesota v. Dickerson 113 S.Ct. 2130 (1993)
Miranda v. Arizona 384 U.S. 436 (1966)
Mitchell, People v. 39 N.Y. 2d 173 (1976)
New York v. Belton 453 U.S. 454 (1981)
Oliver v. United States 466 U.S. 170 (1984)
People v. (see opposing party)
Place, United States v. 462 U.S. 696 (1983)
Rea v. United States 350 U.S. 214 (1956)
Robinson, People v. 97 N.Y.2d 341 (2001)
Roe v. Wade 410 U.S. 113 (1973)
Ross, United States v. 456 U.S. 798 (1982)
Smith, People v. 59 N.Y. 2d 454 (1983)
Tennessee v. Garner 471 U.S. 1 (1985)
Terry v. Ohio 392 U.S. 1 (1968)
Torres v. People 74 N.Y. 2d 224
United States v. (see opposing party)
Watson v. United States 423 U.S. 411 (1976)
Weeks v. United States 232 U.S. 383 (1914)
Whren et al. v. United States 517 U.S. 806 (1996)
Wolf v. Colorado 338 U.S. 25 (1949)

Index

About the Author

JOHN ETERNO has been employed by the New York City Police Department for over 20 years. As Commanding Officer of the Mapping Support Unit, he makes policy recommendations and handles sensitive assignments for the Deputy Commissioner of Strategic Initiatives and the Assistant Commissioner of Programs and Policies. He is an Adjunct Assistant Professor of Sociology at Queens College in New York. He has written book chapters and journal articles on various topics within the field of policing.

CPSIA information can be obtained
at www.ICGtesting.com
Printed in the USA
LVHW081924160123
737235LV00004B/31

9 780275 975920